BUILDING RESILIENCE IN AN UNCERTAIN WORLD

CALM IN CHAOS

CHETAN ITAPE

INDIA · SINGAPORE · MALAYSIA

ISBN
Paperback 979-8-89519-817-9
Hardcase 979-8-89544-829-8

*To all the farmers in the world,
it is your hands that feed us.*

*No matter how technologically
advanced the world becomes,
I can't eat an app for breakfast!*

CONTENTS

Author's Note   vi

Understand the Chaos   xvi

The Venomous "Why Me" Ask   12

"Fake" book   22

"Cell" Phones   30

The Curse Called Comfort   48

The big F, Finance   56

Take These Free!!!!   66

Minimalism   78

The Dead Diet   88

Exercise | Hustle for Muscle   100

Habit Hacks: Your Secret Weapons Against Chaos   118

Meditation | The True Freedom   126

Disciplined to Dominate   134

Gratitude   142

Words Are POWERFUL   152

One Day or Day One   160

The Truth About Skills   170

Don't Mind Your Mind!   180

Who's Your Coffee Mate?   194

Secure The Minimum   204

Timeless Wisdom   210

AUTHOR'S NOTE

In the heart of the mountains, an eagle, a symbol of majesty and power, faces a pivotal moment in its life. This apex predator, once a master of the skies, finds itself grounded by the ravages of time. Its beak, once razor-sharp, is now dulled and brittle. Its claws, instruments of swift death, have grown weak and ineffective. Its feathers, once a testament to its strength and grace, now weigh it down, making flight impossible.

The eagle is at a crossroads. It has two choices: succumb to the inevitability of age and die, or endure a harrowing process of rebirth. The path to renewal is brutal. The eagle must fly to a high mountaintop and isolate itself. There, it will strike its beak against the rock until the old one breaks off, waiting for a new, stronger beak to grow in its place. With this new beak, it will pluck out its old, weakened talons and wait for the new ones to emerge. Then, with these fresh talons, it will pluck out its aged feathers, allowing new, robust feathers to grow. This process is excruciating, filled with pain and solitude, but it is the only path to survival.

Emerging from this gruelling ordeal, the eagle soars once more, living for another 30 to 40 years, embodying a powerful truth: the agony of transformation is the price of renewal and longevity.

Like the eagle, we too face similar moments of choice in our chaotic lives. We can cling to our outdated habits, beliefs, and comforts, letting them drag us down, or we can confront the pain of change. It's a path riddled with discomfort, but it's also the path to true growth and freedom. Be honest and ask these questions to yourself. Are you not aware of what you should be doing at this moment? What should you have done last night instead of endlessly scrolling social media? Are you not aware of your true passion or the things that give you true happiness? When was the last time you were out of breath while running or during an exercise session? When was the last time you witnessed the sunrise amidst nature and filled your heart with it, not your phone? When was the last time you put your phone and laptop on an intentional snooze? Until when is your mind going to manipulate you into cheap dopamine hits to ensure that procrastination remains your best ally?

In just a few years, we all will have departed from this world. The moment your soul leaves your physical form, you become nothing more than a body, reduced to an object devoid of life. The home we poured our fortunes into will soon be inhabited by strangers. The possessions we cherish today will erode, fade, or eventually belong to others. That dream car you once adored will likely find its fate in a junkyard, forgotten and rusting away. Future generations may struggle to recall our names, and in time, even those memories will vanish into obscurity. Our photographs, once treasured, will ultimately be discarded as if they never existed.

When you pause to reflect on this reality, it becomes clear that the pursuits consuming 95% of our thoughts – our relentless chase for material wealth and status – are fleeting and ultimately futile. Recognising this truth empowers us to shift our focus to the present-moment, the only time truly within our control. By embracing this awareness, we can invest our energy into what truly matters: cultivating connections, experiences, and love. In doing so, we free ourselves from the shackles of superficiality and step into a realm of genuine "freedom," one that allows us to live fully and authentically.

Today, the biggest evil is abundance. We are surrounded by so many books, articles, documentaries, people, and their experiences; we end up going through all of this and expect too much from ourselves, only to face visible and invisible burnouts. So basically, it is a vicious cycle of "Read, Try, Give-up, Repeat." We are a species who has moved from the good to the worse in no time. We are trying to control the world over a few clicks, but we do not have any control on our lives, neither do we have any idea of what's happening in our own backyard. We order food that arrives in no time, and we are okay with that food taking a toll on our health because we are "busy." Look around you and identify things, clothing, and gadgets that have no literal meaning of being there. In fact, those were procured to impress the people who have no literal importance in your lives. Look even deeper, inside your brain. Your brain is a three-pound universe that processes an average of 70,000 thoughts each day using 100 billion neurons that connect at more than 500 trillion points through synapses that travel 300 miles per hour. Seventy thousand thoughts? Oh yes, out of which at least 90% of them are repetitive. Why so much cognitive load? Well, because we have signed up for a never-ending race in which we are running like mad bulls, and we have never had a chance to take a pause, reflect, or rethink. But now, it's time. Time to reflect on what is important, what is meaningful, and what we should let go. Time to embrace the fact, "The purpose of life is a life of purpose."

I'm not claiming that after reading this book you'll be able to cure cancer, or you'll be able to make a million dollars, or this is a sure-shot recipe for six-pack abs with no hard work. But, I guarantee you, after reading this book, you will have a clear perspective towards life. This is the only self-help book you will ever need. Also, a few chapters in this book will make you think about why you were carrying on the unnecessary load of unrealistic expectations and lived under burden until now. If you implement the simple prescriptions provided in this book, you'll realise how simple, joyful, yet fulfilling life can be. This book delves into these multifaceted challenges, offering insights and strategies to help us find clarity and purpose amidst the chaos.

Congratulations on picking up this book. This book is your mountaintop. It is a call to break away from the chains of the past, to endure the necessary pain, and to emerge stronger, sharper, and ready to soar above the chaos. The right choices are seldom easy, but they are always within your grasp. Embrace the discomfort, and you will find a life not just of survival, but of flourishing in the face of adversity. Whether you're feeling overwhelmed by the chaos of modern life or just looking for a little guidance, you're in the right place. You don't have to read this book from start to finish. Think of it as a toolkit or a reference guide, where each chapter stands alone, ready to offer you insights and strategies whenever you need them. Flip to any chapter that catches your eye. Each one is designed to provide you with practical tips, heartfelt advice coming out of personal experience and research, and a fresh perspective on how to navigate through this chaotic world. Life doesn't follow a linear path, and neither should your journey through this book. This book is more than just words on a page; it's a companion for your journey towards a calmer, more fulfilling life. Each page is crafted with care to help you find your centre, even amidst the storm. So, dive in. Let the wisdom within these pages inspire you, comfort you, and empower you to live boldly and peacefully. Remember, the goal is not perfection, but progress. Each step you take, no matter how small, brings you closer to a life of balance and serenity. Thank you for allowing me to be a part of your journey. May this book serve as a beacon of hope and a source of strength as you navigate the beautiful chaos of life.

Why, all of a sudden, do you have this book in your hand and you are reading these lines? Maybe there's a divine intervention. This time, you might not have chosen this book; this time the book has chosen you to slow down, to close your eyes, your ears, your mouth, and to just listen to your inner chaos. Remove your fancy Air Pods and tune into the rhythm of your heartbeat. Experience joy in simple things that you have forgotten. It's time to take a detour from those expensive cruise holidays over the Pacific Ocean and go back to the simplest joys of making a paper boat and see it sail peacefully in the humble backwaters where the journey is more important and blissful than the destination.

Embark on this journey of a true, rich life in the real-world where your success is not measured against your bank account, the car you drive, your real estate, or your equity portfolio. Life is awareness and acceptance with no judgements. When you cut loose with things and thoughts which were unintentionally accumulated, you experience true freedom. After that, you are left with significant energy and time for things that truly matter.

Wishing your future self all the very best!

RULES FOR READING THIS BOOK

- **No Straight Lines Here:**

   Feel free to dive in wherever you feel drawn! This book isn't a linear journey; you don't have to read it from cover to cover. Flip through the chapters and start with the topics that resonate with you most.

- **Your Personal Reference Guide:**

   Think of this book as a trusty reference manual. Whether you need a boost in motivation or strategies to tackle chaos, return to the chapters that speak to your current challenges, and revisit them whenever you need.

- **Take Notes Like a Boss:**

   Grab a pen and sticky notes! Jot down thoughts, insights, or questions as you read. Engaging with the content will help cement your understanding and make it uniquely yours.

- **Embrace the Messiness:**

   Just like life, this book isn't perfect! Don't hesitate to highlight, underline, or scribble in the margins. Your raw reactions and reflections are part of the learning process.

- **Mix It Up:**

  Feel free to read multiple chapters at once or skip around. If a particular idea sparks your interest, chase it down! Follow your curiosity, and let it guide your reading experience.

- **Reflect and Digest:**

  After reading a chapter, take a moment to pause and reflect. Consider how the concepts apply to your life and what actions you might take moving forward. This is where real transformation begins.

- **Share the Wisdom:**

  Don't keep your insights to yourself! Discuss your favourite parts with friends or family, or gift a copy of this book to them. Sharing ideas not only deepens your understanding but can inspire others to embark on their own journey of growth.

- **Return Anytime:**

  This book is a living document meant to grow with you. Don't be surprised if you find new meanings or insights upon re-reading sections down the line. Each visit can reveal something fresh and powerful.

Remember, this journey is yours. Approach it with an open mind and a sense of playfulness, and let the pages guide you toward a more meaningful life!

UNDERSTAND THE CHAOS

By the title of this book and my choosing this to be the first chapter of the book, you might have understood that we are going to talk about the chaos that we all are surrounded with under the fancy names like progress, development, or the ever-evolving Earth, etc. For you to squeeze your way out of this chaos and to be able to lead a meaningful life, you must first understand what the chaos is all about. In a world increasingly defined by rapid technological advances, pervasive digital dependence, environmental upheavals, political instability, and unprecedented social pressures, the fabric of our daily lives is woven with threads of chaos. This tumultuous landscape challenges our mental, emotional, and physical well-being, compelling us to navigate a relentless stream of information, balance precarious work-life dynamics, and find our place in a society marked by profound inequality and cultural shifts. Amidst this cacophony, the quest for meaning, stability, and connection becomes ever more critical, prompting a deep exploration into the ways we can cultivate resilience, mindfulness, and a sense of gratitude in the face of relentless change. The relentless pace of technological advancement, societal pressures, environmental concerns, and political instability all contribute to a pervasive sense of chaos. Here are some of the key areas where modern individuals experience turmoil:

Digital Dependence

The ubiquitous presence of smartphones, social media, and the internet has created a culture of constant connectivity. While this has many benefits, it also leads to information overload, digital fatigue, and a blurring of boundaries between work and personal life. Digital dependence has become a defining characteristic of modern life, where individuals rely heavily on smartphones, social media, and the internet for communication, information, and entertainment. This dependence creates a scenario where constant connectivity feels indispensable, often leading to compulsive behaviours such as incessantly checking notifications and engaging in social media. The pervasive use of digital devices blurs the lines between work and personal life, making it difficult to disconnect and causing significant stress and anxiety. Furthermore, the emphasis on virtual interactions over face-to-face connections can erode the quality of personal relationships and foster feelings of isolation. This growing reliance on digital technology underscores the need for a balanced approach to its use, ensuring it enhances rather than detracts from our well-being and real-world connections.

The Pervasiveness of Technology

The pervasiveness of technology in modern society is undeniable, as digital devices and internet connectivity have become integral to virtually every aspect of daily life. From the moment we wake up, our smartphones, tablets, and computers facilitate communication, work, entertainment, and even basic tasks like shopping and banking. This constant connectivity offers unprecedented convenience and access to information, yet it also engenders a dependency that can disrupt traditional social interactions and personal routines. The omnipresence of technology fosters a culture of immediacy and instant gratification, often leading to a diminished capacity for patience and deep, reflective thinking. As we navigate this digitally saturated environment, it becomes crucial to strike a balance, leveraging technological advancements to enhance our lives while mitigating the potential drawbacks of its omnipresence.

Impact on Mental Health

The impact of digital dependence on mental health is profound and multifaceted, as the constant engagement with digital devices and social media platforms can exacerbate feelings of anxiety, depression, and loneliness. The perpetual need to check notifications, stay updated, and compare oneself to others online can erode self-esteem and foster a sense of inadequacy. Additionally, the blurring of boundaries between work and personal life often leads to burnout and chronic stress, as individuals struggle to disconnect and find balance. The blue light emitted by screens can disrupt sleep patterns, contributing to insomnia and other sleep-related issues, which further deteriorate mental well-being. To combat these negative effects, it is crucial to adopt mindful digital habits, prioritise offline activities, and seek professional support when needed to maintain a healthy mental state in an increasingly digital world.

Work-Life Balance

The integration of digital technology into the workplace has revolutionised how we work. Remote work and flexible hours are now possible, thanks to communication tools like email, messaging apps, and video conferencing. Achieving a work-life balance has become increasingly challenging in the digital era, where the lines between professional and personal time are often blurred by the constant connectivity provided by smartphones and the internet. The expectation to be available and responsive at all hours can lead to an intrusion of work responsibilities into personal and family life, creating a relentless cycle of stress and fatigue. This imbalance not only affects physical health, with symptoms such as burnout and exhaustion, but also deteriorates mental well-being, leading to increased anxiety and a sense of being perpetually overwhelmed.

Privacy Concerns

Privacy concerns in the digital era have escalated dramatically as the pervasive use of online platforms, smart devices, and social media has facilitated extensive personal data collection and surveillance. Every interaction, from browsing habits to location data, and even private communications, is potentially recorded and analysed by corporations, governments, and cybercriminals. This omnipresent data gathering raises significant apprehensions about the security and ethical use of personal information. High-profile data breaches, such as those involving major social media platforms and financial institutions, have exposed sensitive information, leading to identity theft, financial loss, and a profound erosion of trust in digital services. Additionally, the practice of targeted advertising, which leverages personal data to influence consumer behaviour, intensifies feelings of vulnerability and manipulation. As individuals become more aware of these risks, the demand for stringent data protection laws and robust cybersecurity measures has grown. However, navigating the complex landscape of privacy in an interconnected world remains a daunting challenge.

Declining Physical Health

In the world we live in today, declining physical health has become an alarming norm rather than an exception. We're surrounded by a toxic blend of sedentary lifestyles, processed foods, and relentless stress. The once vibrant pulse of humanity is now dulled by screens and superficial comforts, leaving our bodies in a perpetual state of disrepair. Our diets, dominated by hybrid crops engineered for yield over nutrition, are a far cry from the wholesome sustenance our ancestors thrived on. Fast foods and packet food culture have replaced home-cooked meals, filling our bodies with empty calories, artificial additives, and harmful preservatives. The convenience of grabbing a quick bite often outweighs the need for balanced, nutritious meals, leading to widespread deficiencies and chronic ailments. As we consume these hollow foods, our muscles weaken, our endurance fades, and the very essence of life ebbs away. This decline isn't just a personal failure; it's a societal epidemic, a collective surrender to the chaos that robs us of our true potential.

Job Insecurity

The gig economy, automation, A.I. and shifting job markets create uncertainty about employment stability. In today's rapidly evolving economic landscape, job insecurity has emerged as a pervasive and pressing concern, casting a shadow of uncertainty over the livelihoods of millions worldwide. Rapid technological advancements, coupled with globalisation and shifting market dynamics, have rendered traditional career paths increasingly precarious, leaving workers vulnerable to displacement and disruption. The rise of automation and artificial intelligence threatens to displace entire industries, while the gig economy fosters a precarious and often unstable employment environment, marked by contingent work arrangements and minimal job security. Moreover, the COVID-19 pandemic has further exacerbated these challenges, amplifying existing inequalities and exposing the fragility of labour markets, as businesses grapple with uncertainty and adapt to new realities. In the face of this uncertainty, workers confront not only the fear of unemployment but also the erosion of benefits, stagnating wages, and limited opportunities for upward mobility. As societies grapple with the ramifications of these seismic shifts, there is an urgent need for innovative policies and systemic reforms to ensure economic resilience and empower workers with the skills and support they need to navigate an uncertain future. Many individuals face precarious working conditions, lack of benefits, and the constant threat of job loss.

Social Media Comparisons

Social media platforms, while connecting people globally, often foster unrealistic comparisons and a sense of inadequacy. The curated perfection displayed online can lead to feelings of envy, low self-esteem, and depression. The curated highlight reels that populate platforms like Instagram and Facebook often present an idealised version of reality, characterised by meticulously crafted images of success, beauty, and happiness. However, beneath the glossy veneer lies a darker reality, where individuals grapple with self-doubt and insecurity as they measure themselves against unattainable standards set by influencers and peers. This relentless cycle of comparison fosters a toxic culture of envy and self-criticism, eroding self-esteem and mental well-being. Moreover, the phenomenon of "doomscrolling" exacerbates these feelings of inadequacy, as users are bombarded with a constant stream of carefully curated content that highlights the achievements and joys of others, magnifying their own perceived shortcomings in comparison. As a result, individuals find themselves trapped in a perpetual cycle of comparison and despair, longing for validation and acceptance in a virtual world that often feels more isolating than connecting. Addressing this pervasive issue requires a collective effort to promote authenticity and empathy online, fostering a culture where vulnerability is celebrated, and comparisons are replaced with compassion and support.

Climate Change

In the throes of the 21st century, humanity faces an existential crisis unlike any before: 'climate change.'

Born from centuries of unchecked industrialisation and unsustainable consumption, this global phenomenon presents an unprecedented threat to our planet's delicate ecological balance. From rising temperatures and extreme weather events to melting ice caps and diminishing biodiversity, the impacts of climate change reverberate across continents, sparing no corner of the Earth. Yet, amidst the dire warnings and daunting challenges, there exists a glimmer of hope—a collective awakening to the urgent need for action. Movements advocating for renewable energy, conservation efforts, and policy reforms are gaining momentum, signalling a shift towards a more sustainable future. However, the window for meaningful change is narrowing, demanding swift and decisive action from individuals, communities, and nations alike. In the face of this monumental challenge, we stand at a crossroads, where our choices today will shape the world of tomorrow for generations to come. The tangible impacts of climate change—extreme weather events, rising sea levels, and environmental degradation—create a constant undercurrent of concern and uncertainty.

Pandemics and Health Threats

In the wake of the COVID-19 pandemic, the world finds itself acutely aware of the looming spectre of infectious diseases and other health threats that have the potential to wreak havoc on a global scale. Beyond the immediate crisis of the coronavirus, we are confronted with a myriad of interconnected challenges, ranging from the resurgence of age-old pathogens to the emergence of novel viruses with pandemic potential. Antibiotic resistance looms as a silent yet potent threat, rendering once-effective treatments ineffective and exacerbating the toll of infectious diseases. Meanwhile, the encroachment of human activity into previously untouched habitats brings humans into closer contact with wildlife, increasing the likelihood of zoonotic spill-over events like those that led to the emergence of COVID-19. Climate change further compounds these risks, altering ecosystems and disrupting the delicate balance of disease vectors, amplifying the spread of illnesses such as malaria, dengue fever, and Lyme disease. Furthermore, non-communicable diseases, such as obesity, diabetes, and mental health disorders, continue to exact a heavy toll on global health, fuelled by lifestyle factors, socioeconomic disparities, and inadequate healthcare systems. As we navigate the complex web of health threats in our interconnected world, bolstering global health infrastructure, investing in research and surveillance, and fostering international cooperation are paramount in safeguarding the well-being of humanity.

Unattainable Housing and Living Costs

In the contemporary socioeconomic landscape, the escalating concerns surrounding housing and living costs, coupled with the spectre of inflation, cast a looming shadow over the aspirations of individuals and families striving for financial stability and security. Skyrocketing real estate prices, fuelled by speculative investment and urbanisation, have rendered homeownership increasingly unattainable for many, particularly in major metropolitan areas where housing affordability reaches crisis levels. Concurrently, rental markets strain under the weight of soaring demand and dwindling supply, pushing rental prices beyond the reach of low- and middle-income earners and exacerbating housing insecurity. Moreover, the creeping spectre of inflation further compounds these challenges, eroding the purchasing power of wages and squeezing household budgets already stretched thin by escalating costs of essential goods and services. As the cost of living outpaces wage growth, individuals and families find themselves grappling with the stark reality of housing instability and financial strain, with profound implications for social mobility and economic well-being. Addressing these interconnected challenges demands a multifaceted approach, encompassing measures to increase affordable housing supply, kerb speculative investment, and mitigate the impacts of inflation through targeted fiscal and monetary policies aimed at fostering inclusive economic growth and prosperity for all.

Now that I've listed the above chaotic topics, do not get overwhelmed by the sheer nature of it. You only need to fix things which are in your control. Nobody is expecting you to be the peace-maker between Russia and Ukraine. What you need to do instead about the problems which are beyond your control is to learn how to make peace with it and develop a positive mindset. To sum it all up, navigating the chaos of modern life requires resilience, adaptability, and a proactive approach to well-being. By acknowledging and understanding the various sources of turmoil, individuals can develop strategies to mitigate their impact and foster a sense of stability and purpose. Whether through technological mindfulness, mental health awareness, environmental activism, or community engagement, finding balance amidst the chaos is essential for a fulfilling and harmonious life.

As we wade through the relentless tide of chaos - be it job insecurity, our tether to digital devices, the lingering shadow of a global pandemic, the relentless barrage of social media, or the urgent cries of a planet in peril - it's natural to feel the weight of the world bearing down on you. But take heart. Amid this storm, you are not powerless. Within these pages lies a beacon of hope, a guide to reclaiming control over the chaos that is within your reach. For those elements beyond your grasp, you will uncover profound methods to cultivate inner peace, allowing you to face the uncontrollable with unwavering serenity. This journey is not just about survival; it's about rising above, finding your strength, and embracing a life where you thrive despite the turmoil. Dive in and discover the power that lies within you to create calm in the chaos.

THE VENOMOUS "WHY ME" ASK

Emma sat on the edge of her bed, her shoulders slumped under the weight of exhaustion and despair. The room around her was dimly lit, the curtains drawn tight to keep out the world outside. She glanced at the clock on her nightstand; it was 2 AM. Sleep had become a distant memory, replaced by endless nights of tossing and turning, haunted by the same unanswered question: "Why me?"

The past year had been a relentless storm. First, she lost her job of fifteen years, a position she had dedicated her heart and soul to, only to be let go without warning. Then, her mother fell ill, a rare and aggressive disease slowly stealing her away. Emma had become her caregiver, balancing hospital visits with the endless paperwork of unemployment. And as if that wasn't enough, her long-term relationship had crumbled under the strain, leaving her feeling more isolated than ever.

One night, the burden became too heavy to bear. She found herself in the small chapel at the hospital, the place where she had taken her mother for solace. She knelt at the pew, tears streaming down her face, her body shaking with sobs. She looked up at the crucifix hanging on the wall, the figure of Christ suffering, and her heart cried out, "Why me, God? Why must I endure all this pain? What have I done to deserve this?"

The chapel was empty, silent, but for her cries. She felt an overwhelming sense of abandonment. "Are you even there?" she whispered, her voice breaking. "Do you even care?"

In that moment of utter despair, an image of her mother came to her mind. Her mother, who despite her illness, always wore a gentle smile and whispered words of comfort to Emma. "We are stronger than we think," her mother would say. "Faith is not about having no doubts, but about pressing on in spite of them."

As Emma's sobs subsided, a quiet calm began to settle over her. She remembered a conversation she had with her mother years ago when she was a child. She had scraped her knee and was crying, and her mother had scooped her up, kissed her forehead, and said, "Sometimes, life is hard, my darling. But we grow through the pain. Every challenge we face is a chance to become stronger, to help others, to shine brighter."

The words resonated with her now in a way they hadn't before. Emma realised that her mother, even in her suffering, had never asked, "Why me?" Instead, she had faced each day with courage and grace. Emma took a deep breath, feeling a spark of strength ignite within her. She understood that while she might never get an answer to her "Why me?" question, she had the power to choose her response to life's challenges.

She stood up, feeling a newfound resolve. She would honour her mother's strength by facing her own battles with the same grace and determination. Emma decided to seek help, to talk to a counsellor, and to reach out to friends she had pushed away in her grief. She would not be defined by her suffering, but by how she overcame it.

In the weeks that followed, Emma began to see small glimmers of hope. She found a part-time job that allowed her to care for her mother and still have a sense of purpose. She reconnected with old friends who welcomed her with open arms, and she started attending a support group for caregivers, where she found solace in the shared experiences of others.

Her mother's health continued to decline, but Emma cherished the moments they had together, finding joy in the simple act of being present. One evening, as she sat by her mother's bedside, holding her hand, her mother opened her eyes and whispered, "I am so proud of you, my brave girl.."

Tears filled Emma's eyes, but this time, they were tears of gratitude. She had found her way through the darkness, not because the questions had been answered, but because she had chosen to find meaning and strength in the journey.

As she walked out of the hospital that night, she looked up at the sky, the stars twinkling like a promise of new beginnings. "Thank you," she whispered, no longer asking why, but embracing the journey ahead with a heart full of hope.

We all have some part of Emma within us, the before one, and the after one as well. It is absolutely normal to fall for self-pity in the world we live in, and it can be challenging at times to look at it from a different perspective until you witness something that shifts your perspective or an event that challenges your thought process. Well, I have suffered from the "why me" inner dialogue too, until one day when I found a very powerful quote that literally popped up in my life from nowhere and it changed the way I think about self-pity. The quote goes like this:

"The wound is the place where the Light enters you."

– Rumi

The quote encapsulates the idea that our deepest struggles and emotional wounds are not just sources of pain, but also opportunities for profound spiritual and emotional growth. It suggests that through our vulnerabilities and hardships, we can gain deeper insights, wisdom, and healing. By embracing our wounds, rather than avoiding them, we open ourselves to the transformative power of resilience, compassion, and spiritual awakening, ultimately finding light and renewal amidst our darkest moments.

Nick Vujicic, born without arms and legs, exemplifies the transformative power of embracing challenges with a positive mindset rather than succumbing to self-pity or asking "why me." Despite facing severe physical limitations and enduring bullying and depression in his youth, Nick chose not to be defined by his circumstances. Instead, he focused on what he could control—his attitude and actions. By shifting his perspective from victimhood to empowerment, Nick became a beacon of inspiration and resilience. Through his motivational speaking and advocacy work, he encourages others to see challenges as opportunities for growth and transformation. Nick's life demonstrates that adversity, instead of being a barrier, can be a catalyst for personal and spiritual development. His story teaches us that dwelling on the question "why me" limits our potential, whereas adopting a positive outlook and taking proactive steps forward can lead to unexpected achievements and profound fulfilment. Helen Keller, Nelson Mandela, J. K. Rowling, Stephen Hawking, and Oprah Winfrey are some more real-life examples of how these legends made a difference when they stopped asking "Why Me" and took charge of the situation.

When life throws us challenges, it's natural to ask, 'Why me?' This question, however, subtly shifts our focus from problem-solving to self-pity. It narrows our perspective, framing us as victims of circumstance rather than active agents in our own lives. 'Why me?' closes doors to possibilities by fixating on the unfairness of a situation, rather than seeking solutions.

This mindset not only limits our thinking but also stifles our ability to thrive. By dwelling on 'why me,' we inadvertently dwell on what we lack or what we perceive as lost opportunities. This fixation can lead to a cycle of negativity where we become trapped in a narrative of victimhood. It blinds us to potential lessons or growth that could arise from adversity.

Moreover, 'why me?' becomes a trap when it fosters a sense of entitlement or injustice. It suggests that life should be fair, that we are owed something better. This expectation can breed resentment and bitterness, further entrenching us in a mentality of helplessness.

To break free from this limiting question, it's crucial to shift our focus towards 'what now?' or 'how can I?' These questions empower us to take action, to seek solutions, and to grow from challenges rather than be defined by them. By reframing our mindset from 'why me?' to 'what can I learn?' or 'how can I overcome this?' we reclaim agency over our lives and pave the way for resilience and personal growth.

You must be wondering why I am telling you all this as if I never asked this question to God. I have, multiple times, in fact every time until I stumbled upon the quote I shared above. I ran away from the house at the age of eighteen and had to spend my first day in a mega city on a bus stop. After many efforts, I found a friend to live with where I shared the ten feet by ten feet room with two other roommates. Today, I have an amazing house that can be a dream for millions. If I had asked God 'why me' when I was living in a small room, God has all the rights to ask me "why you" while I live in this beautiful house. When I started struggling in the city, I had to survive on one meal a day for twenty-two months. Today I eat healthy and nutritious meals. No 'why me' ask here too. I had to walk six miles to and from work as I could not afford a bus ticket, all this struggle from the age eighteen till twenty-three. By the age of twenty-six, I had to travel to countries like Australia, Singapore, the United Kingdom, and the United States of America for work. And there are at least a hundred examples of such ifs and buts, the very recent being while I was writing this book. I lost all my work when I was on page 93 with 19,780 words written. Zipped, nothing, it just disappeared. No 'why me,' I told myself, "maybe God wanted you to write better." I thanked God for giving me the ability to write. With this blessing to be able to write, I can write a hundred drafts with the same sincerity and discipline with a noble cause of helping you all.

Another famous example of someone who did not ask "why me?" but instead took proactive and positive action is Viktor Frankl, a Holocaust survivor, neurologist, and psychiatrist. In his seminal book, Man's Search for Meaning, Frankl recounts his experiences in Nazi concentration camps and how he found meaning in the midst of immense suffering.

Frankl didn't dwell on the question "why me?" but instead focused on how he could find purpose even in the direst circumstances. One of his famous quotes encapsulates this mindset:

"When we are no longer able to change a situation, we are challenged to change ourselves."

Frankl's approach was to search for meaning in suffering and to use it as a way to grow and help others. He developed logotherapy, a form of existential analysis that emphasises finding purpose in life as a central motivational force. His life and work demonstrate how shifting focus from "why me?" to "how can I use this experience?" can lead to profound personal transformation and impact.

By adopting Frankl's perspective, you can learn to transcend your challenges and find deeper meaning and purpose, turning adversity into an opportunity for growth and achievement.

Breaking free from the "why me" mindset begins with a conscious decision to shift focus from victimhood to empowerment. Start by acknowledging your feelings without judgement, recognise the frustration, sadness, or anger that accompanies life's challenges. Once you've named these emotions, deliberately pivot your thoughts towards questions that foster action and growth, such as "What can I learn from this?" or "How can I use this experience to become stronger?" Embrace a mindset of curiosity and possibility, viewing setbacks as opportunities for personal development rather than insurmountable obstacles. Next, set small, achievable goals that lead you out of stagnation and towards progress. Celebrate each step forward, no matter how minor, as a victory. Engage in activities that bring you joy and fulfilment, which can reignite your passion and drive. Surround yourself with a supportive community that encourages your growth and challenges your negative self-talk. Practicing gratitude can also shift your focus from what's wrong to what's right, highlighting the positives in your life. By consistently redirecting your thoughts and actions towards growth and gratitude, you gradually dismantle the "why me" mentality and build a resilient, proactive mindset. Remember, the power to transform adversity into achievement lies within your perspective and actions. Every moment you choose to focus on solutions rather than problems, you move closer to doing something amazing and reclaiming control over your life's narrative.

"FAKE" BOOK

---

*"Social media is a platform for people
to spread lies about themselves"*

– L.G. Davis

'd be surprised if I come across anyone who says that social media is not using them. Yes, you read that right; it is not a typing mistake, I mean it. If you think you are a social media user, no, the social media is using you. There's no other decent or subtle way of saying it, neither am I interested in doing so. Why do you think that an app which takes a huge team to build and needs another huge team to support, and another huge team to keep it running, and billions of dollars in funding will be handed over to you for free? It's not. The social media apps, pages, like-dislike buttons, the notifications, posts, and most importantly, the advertisements are exclusively created, catered, and brilliantly targeted to the audience like you and me to generate sales and traffic for which all these platforms are being paid. So, social media is not the product, the product is YOU. And you are losing time, and money, and the freedom. The freedom of utilising your time the way you want.

We are the product. Every click, every like, every share, every second you spend scrolling, is meticulously tracked and analysed. Our preferences, habits, and even our emotions are sold to the highest bidder. The seemingly endless feed is not just a collection of random posts; it's a carefully crafted tool designed to keep you hooked, to make you crave more. The more you engage, the more data they gather, and the more valuable you become to advertisers. It's a vicious cycle of manipulation and exploitation.

But the price we pay is far more than just the ads we see. It's our mental health, our relationships, our very sense of self. We compare our behind-the-scenes with everyone else's highlight reel, and it's a battle we can't win. We sacrifice sleep for one more scroll, one more video, one more dopamine hit. And for what? To feel more connected? To stay informed? Or is it just to fill a void that grows deeper with every swipe?

In the next section, we'll dive into the dark side of social media - the anxiety, the depression, the loneliness masked by the illusion of connection. We'll uncover the toll it takes on our well-being and ask the hard questions: Is it worth it? Are we in control, or are we being controlled? It's time to face the truth and reclaim our lives from the grips of these digital overlords.

The Thief of Time

The illusion of free access to social media comes at a cost far greater than we realise: our time. We scroll, we tap, we swipe, losing hours to the endless vortex of posts and updates. This time, precious and finite, is stolen from us, never to be reclaimed. We convince ourselves that it's harmless, just a few minutes here and there, but these moments accumulate, turning into hours, days, and even years. Time that could be spent on personal growth, meaningful relationships, upskilling, and real-life experiences is instead sacrificed on the altar of fleeting digital gratification. We are tricked into believing we are in control, but in reality, social media is the puppet master, pulling the strings and robbing us of the most valuable currency we have—time.

The Cognitive Cost of Constant Connectivity

Social media is reshaping our minds, inflicting a cognitive cost that we can no longer ignore. Our attention spans are shrinking, fragmented by the endless barrage of notifications and updates. The deep thinking and focus required for meaningful tasks are replaced by shallow, surface-level engagement. Information overload overwhelms us, making it difficult to discern truth from falsehood in the sea of content. Our memories suffer as we offload mental tasks to digital devices, relying on them to store information we once retained ourselves. Critical thinking takes a backseat to reactive, impulsive responses shaped by the fast-paced digital environment. In our quest for connectivity, we are sacrificing the very essence of our cognitive abilities, allowing social media to hijack our minds and undermine our intellectual potential.

The Silent Saboteur of Mental Health

Social media masquerades as a connector, but beneath its surface lies a silent saboteur of mental health. Each like, share, and comment becomes a validation we desperately seek, binding our self-worth to digital approval. The constant comparison to curated perfection erodes our confidence, fostering anxiety and depression. We chase the next notification, the next fleeting high, only to plummet into deeper lows when reality fails to measure up. Our minds become battlegrounds, assaulted by relentless waves of envy, inadequacy, and fear of missing out. In this ceaseless quest for virtual acceptance, we sacrifice our mental well-being, allowing social media to insidiously dictate our emotions and undermine our peace.

The Physical Toll of Digital Addiction

Our bodies pay the price for our digital addiction, suffering silently as we remain glued to our screens. Hours spent hunched over devices lead to chronic pain in our necks and backs, while the blue light from screens disrupts our sleep patterns, leaving us exhausted and irritable. The sedentary lifestyle fostered by endless scrolling contributes to obesity, heart disease, and a host of other health issues. Eye strain and headaches become constant companions as we navigate the never-ending feed. We trade physical activity for virtual engagement, allowing our health to deteriorate in the name of connectivity. Social media is not just a mental parasite; it's a physical one, slowly eroding our bodies with every swipe and click.

The Erosion of Social Bonds and Behaviour

Social media, under the guise of connecting us, is steadily eroding our social bonds and altering our behaviour in unsettling ways. Face-to-face interactions are replaced by superficial online exchanges, diminishing our ability to form deep, meaningful relationships. The rise of cyberbullying and online harassment spreads like a virus, infecting our interactions with toxicity and fear. We become performers in a digital theatre, curating our lives to fit the expectations of virtual audiences, losing authenticity in the process. The constant need for validation warps our self-perception and fuels a relentless cycle of attention-seeking behaviour. Real-life connections weaken as we become more engrossed in the digital world, allowing social media to reshape our interactions and behaviour in ways that disconnect us from the genuine human experience.

The Perils of Privacy and Security

In the digital age, our privacy and security are the ultimate casualties of social media. We willingly share personal information, unaware of the lurking dangers. Every post, every click, every interaction is meticulously tracked, creating a detailed profile that can be exploited by corporations and cybercriminals alike. Identity theft, data breaches, and unauthorised surveillance become real threats as our digital footprint grows. The false sense of security provided by these platforms masks the grim reality: our personal data is a commodity, bought and sold without our knowledge or consent. We relinquish control over our privacy, exposing ourselves to risks that can have devastating consequences. Social media is not just a platform for sharing; it's a predator in the shadows, waiting to exploit our trust and compromise our security.

Being Mindful and Overcoming Social Media Addiction.

Being mindful of social media use involves recognising its potential pitfalls and taking proactive steps to regain control:

- **Awareness of Time Spent:** Monitor and limit the time spent on social media each day. Set specific boundaries to prevent mindless scrolling. Your "smart" phone can help you set limits; just use it in a smarter way.

- **Purposeful Engagement:** Use social media with intention. Focus on meaningful interactions, and avoid getting caught up in endless feeds.

- **Digital Detox:** Schedule regular breaks from social media to reset and reconnect with offline activities and relationships. I keep my Wi-Fi and social media off each Saturday, and trust me, the day hits different.

- **Mindful Consumption:** Be selective about the content you consume. Unfollow accounts that don't contribute positively to your well-being. Endless scrolling is nothing but a cheap dopamine hit.

- **Physical Boundaries:** Create physical boundaries by designating tech-free zones or times, especially during meals and before bedtime.

- **Seek Support:** If addiction is severe, seek support from friends, family, or professionals. Join support groups or counselling sessions focused on digital wellness.

By cultivating mindfulness and implementing these strategies, we can regain autonomy over our digital lives and mitigate the negative impacts of social media addiction.

"CELL" PHONES

– Anonymous

In today's hyper-connected world, our cell phones have become indispensable tools, seamlessly integrating into every aspect of our daily lives. From morning alarms to social media updates, they keep us informed and entertained, but their omnipresence also poses a significant challenge: cell phone addiction. We often find ourselves ensnared in a relentless cycle of checking notifications, scrolling through endless feeds, and compulsively responding to every ping and buzz. This addiction not only steals away precious moments of our time but also chips away at our ability to focus deeply, restfully sleep, and engage authentically in face-to-face interactions. It's a paradoxical scenario where the very devices designed to connect us can paradoxically leave us feeling disconnected—from ourselves and others. The constant lure of virtual engagement can replace genuine human connections, fostering a superficial sense of social fulfilment while eroding the richness of real-world relationships. Recognising the signs of cell phone addiction—such as heightened anxiety when separated from our devices or the compulsion to check them even in the midst of meaningful moments—is the first step toward reclaiming our autonomy. By cultivating mindfulness around our technology use, setting intentional boundaries, and prioritising genuine human connections, we can regain control over our lives. This journey isn't just about reducing screen time; it's about rediscovering presence, nurturing deeper connections, and reclaiming the moments that truly matter in our increasingly digital existence.

However, overcoming cell phone addiction isn't just about limiting screen time or adopting digital detoxes. It's about reshaping our relationship with technology to align with our values and well-being. By understanding the deeper motivations behind our device usage—whether it's seeking validation, alleviating boredom, or avoiding discomfort—we can cultivate healthier habits that serve us both online and offline. This shift not only empowers us to reclaim our focus and presence, but also prepares us to address the multifaceted challenges that excessive cell phone use can bring into our lives. From diminished productivity and disrupted sleep patterns, to strained personal relationships and mental health concerns, these issues underscore the urgent need for mindful engagement with technology. Imagine for a moment that you are unaware of the myriad challenges posed by our constant companions—our cell phones. These sleek devices, designed to keep us connected and informed, often conceal a host of hidden impacts on our well-being. Let's dive straight into these issues, exploring how excessive cell phone use can disrupt our sleep patterns, diminish productivity, impair social interactions, pose physical health concerns, contribute to mental health issues, and even foster digital addiction. By shedding light on these challenges, we can better understand the complexities of our digital dependence and explore strategies to cultivate a healthier relationship with technology.

Disrupted Sleep Patterns

Raise your hand if you either use your phone before you sleep or check it first thing in the morning, or maybe both. The blue light emitted by cell phones can interfere with melatonin production, a hormone crucial for regulating sleep. This disruption can lead to difficulty falling asleep, staying asleep, or achieving restorative sleep cycles. Many people engage with their phones late into the night, further delaying sleep onset and contributing to fatigue and daytime drowsiness. Over time, chronic sleep deprivation linked to cell phone use can impact cognitive function, mood stability, and overall well-being.

Reduced Productivity

You have paid a fortune or, as they jokingly say, you've sold your kidney to buy this "cell" for yourself, but that doesn't mean you are in life imprisonment. Constant notifications, social media updates, and the lure of endless online content can fragment attention and decrease your productivity. Switching between tasks in response to cell phone alerts can lead to a phenomenon known as "task-switching cost," where cognitive resources are drained, and efficiency declines. In work or study environments, the temptation to check cell phones can disrupt workflow, extend task completion times, and hinder concentration on complex tasks requiring sustained focus.

Impaired Social Interactions

I know few people who live in the same locality or even the same building but prefer phones over in-person communication. Really? Over-reliance on cell phones for communication can diminish face-to-face interaction skills. Excessive texting or social media interactions may replace in-person conversations, reducing opportunities for meaningful connections and empathy development. Misinterpretations of text-based communication can also lead to misunderstandings or conflicts, further impacting interpersonal relationships. This trend is particularly concerning among younger generations who may prioritise digital interactions over direct human engagement. I'd say it again, ditch "reel" and be "real."

Physical Health Concerns

One of the top businesses in the upcoming times will be physiotherapy specialised in ill-postured people due to excessive cell phone usage. Prolonged use of cell phones often results in poor posture and, with repetitive movements, can lead to physical health issues. "Text neck," a condition resulting from prolonged downward head tilting during cell phone use, can cause neck and upper back pain, stiffness, and spinal misalignment. Similarly, excessive screen time can contribute to eye strain, dry eyes, and blurred vision, known collectively as digital eye strain or computer vision syndrome. These physical discomforts can escalate into chronic conditions if not addressed with ergonomic adjustments and regular breaks from cell phone use.

Mental Health Issues

I could not sleep the whole night when I saw a kid based out of India exactly behaving like an Anime character due to continuous exposure to cell phone and digital content, and there are more examples in the world. Excessive cell phone use has also been linked to increased levels of anxiety, depression, and feelings of isolation. Constant connectivity and social comparison on social media platforms can contribute to a sense of inadequacy or FOMO (fear of missing out), exacerbating mental health challenges. The dopamine rush from receiving notifications or likes can create a cycle of reward-seeking behaviour, reinforcing cell phone use as a coping mechanism for emotional distress. Over time, these patterns can erode self-esteem, disrupt sleep, and escalate stress levels.

Digital Addiction

Cell phones can foster addictive behaviours characterised by compulsive checking and use, especially among the younger generation. Similar to substance addictions, digital addiction involves a loss of control over cell phone use, withdrawal symptoms when separated from the device, and neglect of other responsibilities or interests. The constant need to stay connected and updated can consume significant time and mental energy, impacting personal relationships, academic or work performance, and overall life satisfaction. Recognising the signs of digital addiction is crucial for implementing strategies to regain balance and prioritise offline activities for holistic well-being.

Impact on Children

The proliferation of cell phones has profoundly impacted the lives of children, introducing both opportunities and challenges. From an early age, children are exposed to screens that offer instant access to entertainment, educational resources, and social interactions. While this connectivity can enhance learning and communication skills, it also raises concerns about excessive screen time and its effects. Cell phones can disrupt sleep patterns, hinder physical activity, and affect cognitive development if not monitored. Moreover, unrestricted access to digital content can expose children to inappropriate material and cyberbullying, posing risks to their emotional and psychological well-being. Balancing the benefits and risks of cell phone use for children requires thoughtful consideration of age-appropriate guidelines, parental supervision, and fostering healthy digital habits and limits from an early age.

As we navigate the complexities of our digital age, let us not overlook the profound impact of our cell phone habits. These devices, designed to connect us, can also ensnare us in a web of distraction and dependency. Take a moment to reflect: how often do you reach for your phone without a conscious thought? To put it simply, you bought the cell phone with your hard-earned money, and you don't have to answer every call, check every notification, and respond to every email. Additionally, how does it shape your interactions, your focus, and your sense of presence in the world? Consider the moments lost to mindless scrolling and the potential lost connections with loved ones. Challenge yourself to reclaim your time, your attention, and your relationships from the grip of constant connectivity. Let us strive for a balanced approach, where technology serves as a tool for enhancement rather than a barrier to genuine connection and fulfilment. By fostering mindfulness and setting intentional boundaries, we can reclaim agency over our digital lives and rediscover the richness of being truly present in each moment.

Give it a thought, they are called "Cell" phones for a reason!

A FOR ALCOHOL | A FOR ADDICTION

"Drunkenness is nothing but voluntary madness"

– Seneca.

In the relentless rush of modern life, we often find ourselves ensnared by a multitude of addictions, each promising solace yet leading us further into the labyrinth of dependence. The concept of addiction has evolved beyond the confines of substance abuse to encompass a broader spectrum of behaviours and desires that can dominate our existence. From the intoxicating grip of alcohol and drugs to the seductive power of wealth, and the ceaseless quest for more, our lives are filled with potential pitfalls.

Today, we face a new era of addiction that extends to our relationship with technology, social media, and even work. The glow of our screens captivates us, drawing us into a virtual world where validation and distraction are just a click away. Social media platforms feed on our need for connection and approval, often at the expense of our mental health and real-life interactions. Meanwhile, the pursuit of career success and material abundance can become all-consuming, leaving little room for genuine fulfilment and well-being.

This chapter delves into the myriad forms of addiction that permeate our daily lives, shedding light on their origins, mechanisms, and impacts. By understanding these addictive behaviours, we can better navigate the complex landscape of modern living. We will explore the psychological and societal factors that contribute to these addictions and discuss strategies for overcoming them. From recognising the subtle signs of dependence to implementing practical steps for change, this journey will empower you to break free from the chains of addiction and reclaim control over your life. Through awareness and mindful practices, we can find balance and resilience in the face of a world teeming with addictive temptations.

Let's understand the addictions that surround us today:

Alcohol and Drugs

The most recognised form of addiction, alcohol and drugs, continues to have a profound impact on individuals and society. These substances offer a temporary escape from reality, masking pain, stress, and emotional turmoil with fleeting moments of euphoria or numbness. However, the relief they provide is often short-lived, leading to a destructive cycle of dependency that can devastate physical health, mental well-being, personal relationships, and can cost a fortune with respect to money and health.

Alcohol, widely available and socially accepted, can subtly transition from a casual habit to a full-blown addiction. The effects of alcohol abuse are far-reaching, ranging from liver damage and cardiovascular problems to impaired cognitive function and emotional instability. The social acceptance of drinking often blurs the line between moderate consumption and dangerous overindulgence, making it harder for individuals to recognise when they need help.

Drugs, whether illicit or prescription, pose an even greater risk due to their potent effects and potential for dependency. The allure of drugs lies in their ability to alter perception, mood, and consciousness, offering an escape from the pressures of daily life. However, this escape comes at a high cost, leading to severe health issues, legal problems, and the erosion of social and familial bonds. Opioids, stimulants, and sedatives, among others, can quickly ensnare users, creating a relentless pursuit of the next high that overshadows all other aspects of life.

The journey to overcoming alcohol and drug addiction is fraught with challenges, but it is not insurmountable. It begins with acknowledging the problem and seeking support from healthcare professionals, support groups, and loved ones. Treatment options vary, including detoxification, counselling, and long-term rehabilitation programmes, all designed to address the physical and psychological aspects of addiction. Recovery is a continuous process that requires dedication, resilience, and a strong support network.

By shedding light on the nature of alcohol and drug addiction, we can better understand the underlying causes and the devastating impact they have on individuals and communities. This understanding is crucial in fostering compassion and providing effective support for those struggling with these addictions. Through awareness, education, and a commitment to our loved ones, we can break the chains of dependency and pave the way for a healthier, more fulfilling life.

Technology and Social Media

In today's digital age, our relationship with technology and social media has become increasingly complex and often addictive. The glow of our screens captivates us, drawing us into a virtual world where validation, entertainment, and distraction are just a click away. While technology has undeniably revolutionised how we connect, work, and play, its pervasive presence in our lives can lead to a dependency that impacts our mental health, relationships, and overall well-being.

Social media platforms, in particular, feed on our intrinsic need for connection and approval. The instant gratification of likes, comments, and shares creates a dopamine-driven feedback loop, making these platforms incredibly hard to resist. We find ourselves compulsively checking our devices for updates, often at the expense of face-to-face interactions and real-life experiences. The curated nature of social media can also lead to unrealistic comparisons and a distorted sense of self-worth, as we measure our lives against the highlight reels of others.

The addiction to technology extends beyond social media. The constant bombardment of notifications, emails, and updates from our devices keeps us in a state of perpetual distraction. This "always-on" mentality can lead to digital burnout, where the boundaries between work and personal life blur, making it difficult to unplug and recharge. The pressure to stay connected and productive can exacerbate stress, anxiety, and feelings of being overwhelmed.

Recognising and addressing technology and social media addiction is crucial for reclaiming control over our lives. Setting boundaries, such as designated tech-free times and spaces, can help create a healthier relationship with our devices. Mindfulness practices, such as meditation and digital detoxes, can reduce our dependency on technology and enhance our ability to focus on the present-moment. Additionally, fostering real-life connections and activities can provide a more balanced and fulfilling life.

By understanding the addictive nature of technology and social media, we can make conscious choices about how we engage with these tools, which were designed to make our lives easy and not miserable. Through awareness and intentional action, we can navigate the digital landscape with greater mindfulness and resilience, ensuring that technology serves us rather than enslaves us.

Wealth and Materialism

In a society that often equates success with financial prosperity, the seductive power of wealth and the pursuit of material abundance can become all-consuming. This addiction to wealth and materialism is fuelled by a constant barrage of messages from media, advertising, and cultural norms that celebrate affluence and luxury. While financial stability is essential, the relentless chase for more can lead to a never-ending cycle of desire and dissatisfaction, ultimately impacting our mental health, relationships, and sense of fulfilment.

The allure of wealth lies in the promises it holds security, status, and the ability to acquire anything we desire. However, this pursuit can quickly spiral into an obsession where one's self-worth is measured by net worth. The pressure to achieve financial success can lead to overwork, stress, and a neglect of personal well-being and relationships. The desire for material possessions, from the latest gadgets to luxury cars, and expansive homes can overshadow the pursuit of more meaningful and enduring forms of happiness.

Materialism often brings with it a false sense of fulfilment. The initial joy of acquiring new possessions is fleeting, leading to a phenomenon known as the "hedonic treadmill," where we constantly seek new purchases to maintain the same level of satisfaction. Think of your close ones or friends who upgrade to the latest gadgets or cars every year. Dealing with that undue stress, is it really worth it? This relentless pursuit can lead to financial strain, debt, and a perpetual state of wanting more, never feeling truly content or satisfied.

The impact of wealth addiction extends beyond personal well-being, affecting our social dynamics and the environment. It can create a divide between those who have and those who have not, fostering feelings of envy, resentment, and inequality. The environmental cost of unchecked consumerism is also significant, contributing to resource depletion, pollution, and climate change.

Addressing the addiction to wealth and materialism involves a shift in mindset and values. It begins with recognising that true happiness and fulfilment are not solely dependent on financial success or material possessions. Cultivating a sense of gratitude for what we already have, focusing on experiences rather than things, and prioritising relationships and personal growth over monetary gain can lead to a more balanced and satisfying life.

Mindfulness practices and intentional living can help break the cycle of materialism. By being more conscious of our consumption habits and reflecting on what truly brings us joy and fulfilment, we can make more deliberate choices that align with our deeper values and long-term well-being. Simplifying our lives, decluttering, and embracing minimalism are practical steps toward reducing the grip of materialism. Flying first class, business class, or economy class won't change your destination, just food for thought.

Work and Achievement

In our achievement-oriented culture, the addiction to work and success has become increasingly prevalent. Society often glorifies relentless ambition, rewarding those who dedicate their lives to climbing the corporate ladder or reaching the pinnacle of their chosen fields. While hard work and determination are commendable, the obsession with career success can lead to burnout, stress, and the neglect of personal relationships, physical health, and self-care.

The addiction to work, often referred to as workaholism, manifests in various ways. It can involve long hours at the office, constant checking of emails, and an inability to disconnect from professional responsibilities. This constant engagement with work can provide a sense of purpose and accomplishment, but it can also mask underlying issues, such as low self-esteem, fear of failure, or the desire to escape personal problems. Over time, the line between professional and personal life becomes blurred, leading to a state of perpetual busyness that leaves little room for relaxation or leisure.

Achievement addiction goes hand in hand with workaholism. The relentless pursuit of goals and accolades can create a cycle of striving for the next big accomplishment, often at the expense of one's health and well-being. This can lead to chronic stress, anxiety, and a feeling of never being "good enough," regardless of how much is achieved. The societal pressure to constantly excel and outdo oneself can create a toxic environment where rest and self-care are undervalued.

The impact of work and achievement addiction extends beyond the individual. It can strain personal relationships, as time and energy are disproportionately allocated to work, leaving family and friends feeling neglected. It can also lead to a culture of overwork within organisations, where employees feel pressured to conform to unhealthy work habits, to keep up with their peers, or meet unrealistic expectations.

Addressing work and achievement addiction requires a conscious effort to redefine success and establish healthier boundaries. It begins with acknowledging the problem and understanding the motivations behind it. Setting clear boundaries between work and personal life is crucial, such as designating specific times for work and leisure, and creating tech-free zones to avoid constant connectivity.

Cultivating a balanced approach to life involves prioritising self-care and well-being. This can include regular exercise, hobbies, and social activities that provide a sense of fulfilment outside of work. Mindfulness practices, such as meditation and journaling, can help manage stress and foster a deeper connection with oneself.

Organisations also play a crucial role in addressing work addiction. Encouraging a culture of work-life balance, offering flexible work arrangements, and recognising the importance of mental health can help create a more supportive and sustainable work environment.

To conclude, preventing the grip of modern-day addictions requires a proactive and mindful approach to daily life. Developing healthy habits and routines is crucial. Start by setting clear boundaries for work and leisure, ensuring you allocate time for rest and personal activities. Embrace mindfulness practices such as meditation and journaling to stay connected with your inner self and manage stress. Cultivate a balanced relationship with technology by designating tech-free zones and times, and prioritise face-to-face interactions over virtual connections. Practice gratitude to shift focus from material possessions to appreciating what you already have, fostering contentment and reducing the lure of materialism. Engage in regular physical activity, hobbies, and social activities that provide fulfilment beyond professional achievements. Seek support from friends, family, or support groups when needed, and don't hesitate to seek professional help if you find yourself struggling. By integrating these practices into your life, you can build resilience against the temptations of modern-day addictions and lead a more balanced, fulfilling life.

THE CURSE CALLED COMFORT

While you are reading this book, I hope you are not running or in discomfort. So, do not take the literal meaning of the "curse called comfort." But what was the last moment you remember when you were out of breath due to an intentional heavy workout, or do you remember a day where you chose the right way over a comfortable way? For example, you are running out of milk and you need it in a few hours. Provided you have an app which delivers milk to you in minutes, which involves one individual from the online retailer to travel all the way to the fulfilment centre, pick up your order, and deliver it to you. Will you choose the app, or will you do the right thing to just walk across the street and buy the milk from the store? You secretly know what you will choose, and you may present this question to me, what is wrong in that? Nothing, besides you are training your mind to choose comfort repeatedly to a level where your mind is on auto-pilot to choose comfort even when it is wrong, expensive, incorrect, and not good for you in the longer term. Right now, my mind is asking me to shut down the laptop and watch my favourite TV show, while the right thing to do is to continue writing as I'm in such a good flow.

Our generation and for future generations to come, we are surrounded by many people and companies who want to make it big in quick commerce, and we have to make a cautious choice for nobody else but ourselves.

The Problem with Comfort

Choosing comfort over what is right in the longer run can lead to a multitude of problems that extend far beyond immediate gratification. At its core, this decision reflects a prioritisation of short-term convenience or personal ease over principles, ethics, or the greater good. While it may offer temporary relief from discomfort or difficulty, such choices often come with significant long-term consequences, both for individuals and society as a whole. On a personal level, prioritising comfort over what is right can erode your integrity, self-respect, and sense of fulfilment, fostering a pattern of complacency and moral compromise that undermines personal growth and fulfilment. Moreover, it can perpetuate a cycle of avoidance and denial, preventing us from confronting challenges or addressing underlying issues that may be impeding their progress or well-being.

Beyond the individual level, the ramifications of prioritising comfort over what is right can ripple outwards, impacting relationships, communities, and even the broader social fabric. In interpersonal dynamics, this choice may strain trust, erode empathy, and undermine the foundations of meaningful connections, as individuals prioritise self-interest over mutual respect and understanding. In organisational or institutional contexts, it can foster a culture of negligence, corruption, or apathy, where short-term gains take precedence over long-term sustainability or ethical considerations, leading to systemic dysfunction, injustice, or harm.

From a societal perspective, the cumulative effect of widespread comfort-seeking behaviour can be profound, shaping the norms, values, and priorities of entire communities or cultures. When individuals or institutions consistently prioritise comfort over what is right, it can perpetuate systemic injustices, exacerbate social inequalities, and undermine collective efforts to address pressing challenges, such as environmental degradation, poverty, or human rights abuses. Moreover, it can contribute to a broader erosion of trust in institutions, weakening social cohesion and resilience in the face of adversity.

In essence, choosing comfort over what is right in the longer run represents a short-sighted approach that sacrifices integrity, growth, and collective well-being for the sake of immediate ease or convenience. While it may offer temporary relief from discomfort or uncertainty, the long-term consequences can be far-reaching and detrimental, undermining personal integrity, eroding social cohesion, and impeding progress towards a more just, sustainable, and fulfilling future.

Comfort and Our Brains

Comfort is closely tied to the functioning of our brain, particularly through the brain's reward system and the concept of homeostasis.

Reward System: The brain's reward system, primarily governed by neurotransmitters such as dopamine, plays a central role in our experience of comfort and pleasure. When we engage in activities or behaviours that promote comfort, such as eating delicious food, resting in a cosy environment, or engaging in familiar routines, our brain releases dopamine, a neurotransmitter associated with feelings of reward and satisfaction. This reinforces the behaviour and motivates us to seek similar sources of comfort in the future.

Homeostasis: The brain constantly strives to maintain a state of balance, or homeostasis, to ensure optimal functioning of the body and mind. Comfort, in many ways, represents a state of equilibrium where our physiological and psychological needs are met, and we experience a sense of well-being. When we encounter situations that disrupt this equilibrium, such as stress, discomfort, or uncertainty, the brain may perceive these as threats to homeostasis and trigger physiological responses aimed at restoring balance.

Habit Formation: Comfort-seeking behaviours often become ingrained as habits through the brain's neuroplasticity – the ability to adapt and reorganise in response to experiences and environmental stimuli. When we repeatedly engage in activities that provide comfort or relief from discomfort, neural pathways associated with those behaviours are strengthened, making them more automatic and less effortful over time. This can lead to a habitual tendency to prioritise comfort-seeking behaviours, even when they may not align with our long-term goals or values.

Emotional Regulation: Seeking comfort can also serve as a coping mechanism for regulating emotions and managing stress. Engaging in comforting activities, such as listening to soothing music, practicing mindfulness, or seeking social support, can help alleviate negative emotions and promote a sense of calm and security. This emotional regulation is mediated by complex interactions between brain regions involved in processing emotions, such as the amygdala and prefrontal cortex.

Overall, the connection between comfort and the brain underscores the fundamental role of neurobiology in shaping our behaviours, emotions, and subjective experiences. By understanding how our brain responds to comfort and discomfort, we can gain insight into the mechanisms driving our behaviour and cultivate a more nuanced awareness of our choices and motivations.

Leave Comfort Comfortably

I'd not say you can leave this curse called comfort so easily or comfortably, as it involves breaking the old, ingrained pathways, a decision-making system that is on auto-pilot and chooses comfort at all costs, and going against your own brain, which is not easy. After all, it is not easy to get someone to do twenty push-ups in the morning miraculously when the same person has always bent down on the floor only to pick up the remote to turn on the TV, to later crash on his couch, and not move from there for at least a few hours.

Breaking free from the pattern of choosing comfort over what is right requires a deliberate and introspective effort to re-evaluate priorities, values, and behaviours. Here are some steps to help navigate this process:

Self-awareness and reflection: Start by honestly examining your thoughts, emotions, and motivations when faced with decisions. Reflect on past choices where you may have prioritised comfort over what you knew was right. Understand the underlying reasons behind these choices, such as fear, insecurity, or convenience, and take conscious efforts to change them if needed.

Identify values and principles: Clarify your core values and principles that guide ethical behaviour and decision-making. Ask yourself what truly matters to you and what you stand for. This clarity can serve as a compass to navigate moral dilemmas and prioritise what is right over what is comfortable. For example, ask yourself whether you should cook a fresh meal, or if a leftover pizza is what you should eat, and listen to how your mind manipulates you and make a shift.

Challenge comfort zones: Recognise that growth and meaningful change often lie beyond the boundaries of comfort zones. Embrace discomfort as a catalyst for personal development and moral integrity. Practice stepping outside of familiar routines and habits to confront challenges and make choices aligned with your values. And remember, start small, let your brain make peace with it, and gradually move forward.

Practice mindfulness: Cultivate present-moment awareness to observe your thoughts, feelings, and impulses without judgement. Mindfulness can help you pause and respond intentionally, rather than react impulsively, when faced with difficult decisions or temptations to choose comfort over what is right.

Seek support and accountability: Surround yourself with supportive individuals who share your values and encourage ethical behaviour. Engage in open and honest conversations with trusted friends, mentors, or counsellors about your struggles and aspirations. Accountability partners can provide guidance, encouragement, and accountability as you strive to make more principled choices.

Set realistic goals: Break down larger aspirations into manageable steps and set specific, achievable goals to cultivate a mindset of integrity and ethical behaviour. Celebrate small victories along the way, and learn from setbacks without self-judgement.

Practice empathy and compassion. Cultivate empathy and compassion for yourself and others as you navigate the complexities of ethical decision-making. Recognise that everyone faces challenges and struggles, and approach yourself and others with kindness and understanding.

Embrace imperfection: Accept that embracing a mindset of integrity and ethical behaviour is a journey characterised by growth, learning, and occasional setbacks. Embrace imperfection as a natural part of the process and commit to continuous self-improvement and self-reflection.

By embracing self-awareness, values-driven decision-making, and a willingness to step outside of comfort zones, you can gradually shift away from the mentality of choosing comfort over what is right and cultivate a mindset of integrity, authenticity, and moral courage.

THE BIG F, FINANCE

You need to buy a new car. Your car is way too old, like three long years old, with a whopping FIFTEEN THOUSAND miles on it. Are you getting the point? Nowadays, we have new-age cars, more powerful, loaded with features. Some even have automatic transmission and some are electric, with features like wireless Android and Apple CarPlay, tyre pressure monitoring systems, ADAS, etc. Your car doesn't even have a loan on it anymore; you cleared it way back. Look at Adrian; he just booked a new one from Honda, so should you. Now, pick up the phone, dial Adrian, take the number of this dealership, and pay a visit in the afternoon without any further delay. It's Sunday; book writing can wait. In fact, you can mention the experience of your new car somewhere in any of your books. So, go visit the dealership, plan a dinner with Adrian, talk about the car, the pricing, and what other accessories he got installed. After all, you are working so hard, and you never know what the future holds. Once you start paying for your son's higher education, your new car will remain a dream.

So, what is the point in earning if you cannot even afford a new car to make your life more COMFORTABLE?

Nope, I'm not trying to build any fiction out here. What you read above is my mind speaking to me a while ago, unfiltered. Before a few hours of the above conversation, I had a similar conversation about a new smartphone, a new kindle, and a new smartwatch. Then, a new wireless headphone advertisement popped up while I was checking emails. Is it normal to have these thoughts? Well, yes. We are surrounded by a number of mediums that are specially crafted and polished in a way that they make us feel we are lagging behind and we lack something. These marketing companies are spending millions of dollars on ads for different mediums, different screen sizes, different orientations, and then carefully targeting the perfect audience – that's you.

Understanding the difference between your needs and wants is the fundamental clarity you must gain to attain financial freedom. For example, buying a car is your need (if you don't have one already). But what you want may have no end; your wants can take you places. Your car should have a six-cylinder engine, a Bose music system, ambient lighting, massage, and ventilated seats.

The list goes on until a point where you can go bankrupt and yet not be satisfied, simply because you are catering to the ever so hungry section, your wants. You need to travel because humans are not supposed to live in one place, but you want to fly business class for those Instagram stories. This is something that is not letting you move forward. You need to walk, run, or exercise for which you can need a basic pair of shoes, but you want Nike Alpha Fly.

Do you really need it? No, but we are being trained that way for a long time, initially by televisions, and now by social media advertisements. Why am I telling you all this, which I should write in the Social Media chapter? Because your finance these days has become a leakage beyond repair. If you don't believe me, test this.

Do you keep a journal of your expenditure each month? Do you keep a list of your income vs expenses and tally these two? Have you ever analysed the expenses at the end of the month? If the answer to all these questions is yes, good going. Now, take a look at your journal and calculate the percentage of how much money you are spending on groceries against your overall income. When I realised this, I had a number of 9%. Yes, I was spending only 9% of my total income on groceries, food that keeps me alive and healthy. Yet, no answer to where the rest 91% is going with no investments or savings to account for because they were never there.

I've heard people saying that they find gyms expensive, but they spend five times that amount each month on dining out and alcohol. Are we really thinking about what's happening inside the bank and our personal finance? Credit cards, spend now, pay later (with interest that will cost you a fortune). Just fill up a trolley bag in any store of your choice or even at the airports and just swipe. These days, you don't even have to swipe, just "tap-n-go" – that's how they market these cards nowadays.

How CONVENIENT? The vicious cycle of borrowing credit will never end until you cut all the credit cards and throw them away or stop thinking of credit cards as a preferred payment option. Reward points and complimentary airport lounge visits are a gimmick.

Generally, credit card companies pay you one reward point for spending at least a hundred times that amount, which is not a financially sound proposal for you.

Today, overspending is effortless, and financial pitfalls are ubiquitous. We must adopt a proactive and disciplined approach to managing our finances and expenses. Here are some key strategies to achieve financial stability and avoid the trap of overspending:

Create a Budget: Establish a detailed budget that outlines your income, essential expenses, savings goals, and discretionary spending. A budget serves as a roadmap, helping you track your financial inflows and outflows, and identify areas where you can cut unnecessary costs. Stick to your budget rigorously, adjusting it as needed to reflect changes in your financial situation.

Prioritise Saving: Don't save what is left after spending, spend what is left after saving. Treat savings as a non-negotiable expense rather than an afterthought. Aim to save a specific percentage of your income each month and consider automating your savings to ensure consistency. Establish an emergency fund to cover unexpected expenses and contribute regularly to long-term savings and retirement accounts.

Be an Intelligent Investor: Planning investments effectively is crucial for building wealth and achieving long-term financial goals. Begin by setting clear, measurable financial objectives, such as retirement, buying a home, or funding education, which will guide your investment strategy. Assess your risk tolerance to determine the appropriate mix of asset classes—stocks, bonds, mutual funds, real estate, or other investment vehicles–ensuring a diversified portfolio that balances potential returns with acceptable levels of risk. Educate yourself on the basics of investing, including market trends, economic indicators, and the principles of compound interest, to make informed decisions. Regularly review and adjust your portfolio to reflect changes in your financial situation, market conditions, and goals.

Consider seeking advice from a certified financial planner or investment adviser who can provide personalised guidance and help you navigate complex investment choices. Additionally, take advantage of tax rebates or long-term tax-free returns to maximise your investment returns and achieve optimal tax efficiency. By adopting a disciplined and informed approach to investing, you can build a robust financial future and secure your financial well-being.

Track Your Spending: Monitor your spending habits closely using financial apps or spreadsheets. I use the Money Manager app and make real-time entries of even the smallest purchases with memos under the respective category. It helps me understand and tally where my money is going, and identify patterns of overspending to avoid them in the future. It is also a good idea to take a closer look at your financial statements to check if there are any hidden charges. Regularly review your financial statements to stay informed about your spending behaviour and make necessary adjustments.

Distinguish Wants from Needs: Distinguishing needs from wants is essential for effective financial management. Needs are essentials like food, shelter, healthcare, and basic clothing necessary for survival and daily functioning, while wants are non-essential items that enhance comfort and enjoyment, such as dining out or luxury goods. To differentiate, assess the immediate necessity, long-term impact, frequency of use, and essential functions of each expense. Prioritise needs in your budget and practice mindful spending by pausing before purchases to reflect on their necessity.

Evaluate whether an item or service is necessary for your immediate survival or well-being. For example, groceries and rent are needs, whereas dining at a restaurant or upgrading to a premium streaming service are wants. Ask yourself if you can manage without it in the short-term. Before making a purchase, pause and ask yourself if it is a need or a want. Reflect on why you want to make the purchase and whether it aligns with your financial goals.

This mindfulness can help you make more intentional and informed spending decisions. Identify the essential functions that the item or service provides. For example, basic clothing to keep you warm is a need, while designer clothing for fashion purposes is a want. Similarly, a basic phone for communication is a need, but the latest smartphone with advanced features is likely a want. Regularly review your budget, adjust spending habits, and seek external input to ensure you're aligning with your financial goals. This approach helps allocate resources appropriately, prioritising essential expenses and supporting long-term financial stability.

Avoid Impulse Purchases: Resist the temptation of impulse buying by implementing a waiting period before making non-essential purchases. Give yourself time to consider whether the item is truly necessary and fits within your budget. This practice helps kerb impulsive spending and encourages more deliberate, thoughtful purchasing decisions.

Best Rest "Insured": First things first. Insurance is the fundamental need for you and your loved ones; it is the base of your financial pyramid. Insurance plays a crucial role in safeguarding you and your family against unforeseen financial hardships. It provides a safety net by covering significant expenses arising from accidents, illnesses, natural disasters, and other unexpected events. Health insurance ensures access to necessary medical care without the burden of exorbitant costs, while life insurance offers financial security to dependents. Home and auto insurance protect against property loss or damage, ensuring that recovery is financially manageable.

By mitigating risks and providing peace of mind, insurance allows us to navigate life's uncertainties with greater confidence, protecting your assets, health, and financial future. When you are planning your insurance, be wise and seek professional help if needed. Do not think of the insurance premiums as a burden or an overhead. You must invest in the right insurance if you do not want any situation to dig a hole into your savings or investment portfolio.

Use Credit Wisely: While credit cards can offer convenience and rewards, they can also lead to significant debt if not managed responsibly. Use credit cards judiciously, paying off the full balance each month to avoid interest charges. Avoid relying on credit for daily expenses, and large purchases that you cannot afford to pay off promptly.

Live Within Your Means: Adopt a lifestyle that reflects your financial reality rather than succumbing to societal pressures or the desire to keep up with peers. Focus on living within your means by making cost-effective choices, such as cooking at home, seeking affordable entertainment, and avoiding unnecessary luxury purchases.

Plan for the Future: Establish clear financial goals and create a plan to achieve them. Whether it's buying a home, funding education, or planning for retirement, having specific objectives helps guide your financial decisions and motivates disciplined saving and spending. Regularly review and adjust your goals as needed.

Seek Financial Education: Invest time in learning about personal finance through books, online resources, workshops, or consulting with financial advisers. Understanding financial principles, such as budgeting, investing, and debt management, empowers you to make informed decisions and navigate financial challenges effectively.

Cultivate Financial Discipline: Develop habits of financial discipline by setting limits on spending, avoiding high-interest debt, and consistently saving for the future. Practice self-control and resilience in the face of financial temptations and challenges, reinforcing positive financial behaviours over time.

By adopting these strategies, you can navigate the complexities of today's financial landscape, avoid the pitfalls of overspending, and build a foundation of financial stability and security.

TAKE THESE FREE!!!!

Of all the chaos we discussed in the first chapter, you can either overcome or make peace with almost all of them using these FREE things, and they are free for real.

I read somewhere, "There are no free lunches in the world," but who cares? Unlike the 80s, survival is not the concern anymore. The real concern is we are forgetting what we need irrespective of the price. In this chapter, let's talk about all things which are free and are the most essential for our existence, our well-being, and are an absolute must to nurture our soul. Since the rise of humans, we have never valued free things. Let me share my personal example with you. When I was in twelfth standard, getting tuitions for such an advanced level of mathematics was a challenge in my small town. We only had two professors who were the best in their zone. There were no seats left for students with either of them to attend these classes. But, in my case, one of the professors was my father's close friend. The professor not only offered me to attend the classes, but he did not charge a dime for it. Result? I never took mathematics or the professor seriously; later I left mathematics and chose geography.

Another one, if I'd give this book to you for free, what are the chances you'll read it? How many of you read the free PDFs or white papers which you get either free or at the cost of sharing your email ID?

Similarly, we still have some free things in the universe as of now, which can be utilised to regain our health and well-being. Unlike the immature me in the above example, let's value them and use them to the fullest for our own benefit.

Love and it's Transformative Power

Love is a profound and essential part of the human experience, transcending boundaries and time. It shapes our lives, enhancing our well-being and quality of life. At its core, love provides connection and a sense of belonging, whether through family bonds, friendships, or intimate partnerships. This emotional anchor helps us navigate life's challenges, offering solace and reassurance.

Love fuels personal growth and self-discovery, encouraging us to be our true selves. It inspires us to dream and achieve our goals, driven by the desire to reciprocate the support we receive. Additionally, love motivates acts of kindness and compassion, fostering community and empathy.

The benefits of love are well-documented, with studies showing that those in loving relationships experience lower stress, better mental health, and longer lifespans. Love enriches our lives with warmth, resilience, and fulfilment.

In essence, love is the heartbeat of life, weaving together the fabric of our existence. Embracing all forms of love—romantic, platonic, familial, and self-love—transforms our lives and contributes to a more compassionate world. So, whether with your partner, kids, parents, siblings, or friends, never miss a chance to express your love through words and actions.

Sleep: The Restorative Power of a Good Night's Rest

Sleep is a critical component of overall health and well-being, far beyond a simple shutdown of the body. It's a dynamic period of restoration that affects every aspect of life.

Physically, deep sleep is when the body repairs itself, regenerating cells, growing and repairing muscles, and healing tissues. The immune system becomes more active, fighting infections, and reducing inflammation, which prevents chronic diseases and promotes longevity.

For brain health, sleep is essential. It clears toxins and waste products accumulated during the day, particularly through the lymphatic system, which is crucial for cognitive functions, memory improvement, and protection against neurodegenerative diseases, like Alzheimer's.

Cognitively, sleep is indispensable for learning and memory consolidation. REM sleep processes information from the day, converting short-term memories into long-term ones, enhancing problem-solving skills, creativity, and decision-making abilities. Lack of sleep impairs these functions, reducing concentration, alertness, and complex task performance.

Emotionally, sleep regulates mood by balancing neurotransmitters and stress hormones. Adequate sleep promotes emotional resilience, reducing mood swings, anxiety, and depression. Chronic sleep deprivation is linked to mental health issues, underscoring the need for consistent, quality sleep for emotional well-being.

Sleep also enhances daily life by improving social interactions, mood, patience, productivity, and creativity. Good sleep hygiene is essential: maintain a regular sleep schedule, create a restful environment, adopt pre-sleep routines like reading or meditating, and avoid screens, caffeine, and heavy meals before bed. Use the bedroom solely for sleeping to fully benefit from restorative sleep. Finally, do not develop the habit of thinking about the future, past, or tomorrow, or a long-pending problem; nothing is going to change overnight.

In short, sleep is a fundamental necessity, revitalising the body, sharpening the mind, and soothing the soul. By prioritising sleep, we unlock its myriad benefits, leading to a healthier, happier, and more productive life. The key to a vibrant life lies in valuing sleep above distractions, making it your well-being partner.

Sunshine: The Benefits of Sunlight

Sunshine, often seen as a natural elixir, is vital for our overall well-being, offering numerous benefits for both physical and mental health. Sunlight triggers the production of vitamin D in our skin, essential for healthy bones and teeth, and helps prevent conditions like osteoporosis and rickets. Adequate vitamin D levels also reduce the risk of certain cancers, autoimmune diseases, and cardiovascular conditions.

Mentally, sunlight boosts mood by increasing serotonin levels, helping combat seasonal affective disorder (SAD) and promoting emotional stability. It also regulates circadian rhythms, improving sleep patterns, cognitive function, immune response, and overall mood. Sunlight enhances the immune system by boosting white blood cell production and has therapeutic benefits for skin conditions like psoriasis and eczema through UV light therapy. Sun exposure encourages outdoor activities, which benefit cardiovascular health, muscle strength, and overall fitness, while promoting social interaction and relaxation.

To sum up, sunshine enriches our lives by boosting vitamin D, enhancing mood, regulating sleep, and promoting physical activity. By enjoying the sun responsibly, you can harness its benefits and improve your quality of life.

Fresh Air: The Vitality of Clean Air

In our urbanised world, the simple pleasure of breathing fresh air is often overlooked, yet it is crucial for good health and well-being. Fresh air revitalises our bodies, sharpens our minds, and refreshes our spirits.

One immediate benefit is its positive effect on respiratory health. Clean air allows our lungs to function optimally, increasing blood oxygen levels, which energises cells and enhances vitality. In contrast, polluted air can cause respiratory issues, like asthma and bronchitis.

Fresh air also benefits the cardiovascular system. Increased oxygen intake improves heart function, circulation, and lowers blood pressure, reducing the risk of heart disease and enhancing physical endurance.

Mentally, fresh air acts as a natural tonic, improving cognitive function, concentration, and mental clarity. It alleviates stress and anxiety, promoting relaxation through deep, rhythmic breathing. Fresh air boosts the immune system by stimulating white blood cell production and destroying harmful bacteria and viruses.

Additionally, fresh air contributes to better sleep quality by regulating sleep-wake cycles, promoting deeper and more restorative sleep. Spending time outdoors helps reset our internal clocks, improving sleep patterns essential for overall health.

Fresh air encourages physical activity and social interaction, providing a natural setting for exercise and fostering social connections. Parks, forests, mountains, and beaches offer some of the cleanest air. Even urban green spaces can provide pockets of freshness.

Overall, fresh air is vital for a healthy life, impacting physical health, mental clarity, emotional well-being, and social interactions. By making a conscious effort to breathe in fresh air and spend time in nature, we can enhance our lives profoundly and lastingly. Embracing clean air is a simple, yet powerful step towards a healthier and more balanced existence.

Laughter: The Healing Power of Joy

Laughter, often called the best medicine, is a universal language of joy that enhances health and well-being. It transcends cultural barriers, connecting people through shared happiness and offering numerous physical, emotional and social benefits.

Physically, laughter stimulates the heart and lungs, improves oxygen intake, boosts energy, and promotes vitality. It triggers the release of endorphins, reducing pain and creating a sense of well-being. Laughter also lowers stress hormones like cortisol and adrenaline, reducing blood pressure, muscle tension, and the harmful effects of chronic stress. This relaxation response enhances immune function, making us more resilient to illness.

Mentally, laughter improves mood, combats anxiety and depression, and increases serotonin production, fostering happiness and relaxation. It encourages a positive outlook, enhancing problem-solving abilities and creativity by promoting a light-hearted approach to challenges.

Emotionally, laughter strengthens resilience, provides a healthy emotional outlet, and reduces feelings of loneliness and isolation through shared laughter. This bonding builds strong, supportive relationships, essential for emotional health.

Socially, laughter fosters camaraderie, breaks down barriers, and promotes unity and cooperation. It improves communication, teamwork, and creates a positive environment in personal and professional settings.

Shared laughter builds trust and deepens relationships, making interactions more enjoyable and meaningful.

Laughter also encourages physical activity by engaging various muscles, increasing heart rate, and circulation, mimicking some benefits of aerobic exercise.

To incorporate more laughter, seek opportunities for humour and joy by spending time with loved ones, occasionally indulging in funny content, reading humorous books, and engaging in playful activities. Cultivating a playful attitude helps make laughter a natural part of life.

Finally, laughter is a potent remedy for life's challenges, healing, uplifting, and connecting us. Embracing laughter enhances physical health, mental clarity, emotional well-being, and social bonds, providing a refreshing antidote to stress and reminding us of life's simple joys.

Nature: The Healing Power of the Great Outdoors

Nature's beauty and serenity profoundly impact our well-being, offering a sanctuary for healing and renewal. Immersing ourselves in nature reduces stress, promoting relaxation through calming sights, sounds, and smells that lower cortisol levels. Fresh air revitalises our bodies, sunlight boosts mood and vitamin D levels, and water soothes and refreshes us.

Nature enhances cognitive function, improving concentration, creativity, and problem-solving skills by providing a peaceful environment, free from modern distractions. Emotionally, nature offers solace and healing, inspiring awe and reminding us of life's interconnectedness.

It provides space for introspection and perspective on our lives.

Socially, nature strengthens relationships through shared outdoor activities, fostering bonding and lasting memories. Experiencing nature firsthand also deepens our commitment to environmental conservation and sustainability, encouraging us to adopt eco-friendly practices and advocate for the planet.

In conclusion, nature enriches our lives by promoting physical health, mental clarity, emotional well-being, and social connections. Embracing nature's beauty and cultivating a deeper connection to the Earth allows us to experience its transformative power and the profound benefits it offers.

Friendship: The Bonds That Sustain Us

Friendship enriches our lives through shared experiences, mutual trust, and unconditional support, providing companionship, laughter, and solace. True friends accept us as we are, creating a safe space for authenticity and vulnerability, forming the foundation of strong, enduring bonds.

Friendship brings joy and laughter, filling our hearts with warmth through shared experiences and inside jokes. It also offers strength and support during tough times, with friends standing by us, providing encouragement and perspective, helping us navigate challenges with resilience.

Friendship fosters personal growth, inspiring us to pursue our passions and reach our full potential, through constructive feedback and unwavering support. Socially, it creates a sense of belonging, transcending boundaries and fostering unity and understanding in our communities.

The impact of friendship extends beyond individuals, inspiring acts of kindness and generosity that spread throughout communities. By nurturing these bonds, we contribute to a more compassionate and connected world.

In conclusion, friendship is a priceless treasure, offering joy, strength, and belonging. True friends guide us through life's challenges and enrich our lives, creating a lasting legacy of love and connection.

Music: The Universal Language of the Soul

Music, with its enchanting melodies and stirring rhythms, transcends language, culture and geography, touching the depths of our souls and awakening emotions beyond words. It is a timeless art form that offers solace, inspiration and joy, profoundly impacting our lives and the world around us. Music evokes memories, stirs emotions and connects us to the universal human experience, providing comfort and strength in times of celebration or mourning.

The benefits of music for our well-being are extensive. It reduces stress, anxiety, and depression, promoting relaxation and improving mood. The soothing effect of rhythmic patterns and harmonious melodies lowers cortisol levels, inducing calm and tranquillity. Music can heal and uplift us, from soft lullabies to upbeat tunes.

Music also fosters community and belonging, bringing people together through shared experiences like concerts, parties, or playing in bands. It unites diverse individuals in joy and celebration, transcending differences of age, race and background.

As a form of self-expression and creativity, music allows us to connect with our innermost thoughts and emotions. Composing, playing instruments, or singing enables personal growth and self-discovery, giving voice to our deepest fears, hopes, and dreams.

Music's transformative impact extends to society and culture. It inspires social change, challenges the status quo, and promotes empathy and understanding. Protest songs, anthems, and pieces celebrating diversity can shape hearts and minds, bringing about positive change.

In conclusion, music is a universal language that enriches our lives and the world. By embracing its transformative power and sharing its beauty, we can create a more harmonious, compassionate, and connected world.

These things enrich our lives in profound ways and remind us that not everything of value comes with a price tag.

Additionally, there are a few more things that are free, like exercise and meditation, which are developed as separate chapters later in this book.

MINIMALISM

hy? Well, the question might seem short and insignificant, especially to those who are consciously or unconsciously in the pursuit of an endless goal or an aimless life. How much is enough? For me, it started back in 2017 when my son was born, and we were ready to welcome our baby home, and I wanted to spend some time clearing some space from my wardrobe for the clothing and related accessories for the little one. I started emptying my wardrobe, all sections, one by one. When I was about halfway through, I had to stop as I did not have any space to keep my clothes anywhere; the entire bed and the side tables were full, rather overloaded with my NEVER USED clothing and accessories, and that is where this feeling of being overstuffed struck me hard. I stopped whatever I was doing and made some tea (again choosing one cup out of the fifty odd ones I had), grabbed a chair to sit because I had no space to sit anywhere. I had my tea looking at the loads of clothes I had accumulated over the years. I will never be able to forget these visuals in my life; evening time, it started getting dark, I'm sitting with a cup of tea in my hand taking a deep look at this mess.

After I was done with my tea, I started trying the clothes one by one. To my disappointment, most of them were short, old with their tags on, faded, or out of fashion. Mind you, I had gathered all these clothes from all over the world: Melbourne, Singapore, London, USA, Europe, and from many more that I can't even remember. These were some of the most premium clothing brands on the planet. Of course, I did compare and made a list of clothing and accessories along with their price. Roughly what I remember is eighteen trousers, thirty-three shirts, sixty pairs of socks, twenty-two t-shirts, and five cardigans, five suits, all unused kept in the bags they were purchased in.

If you think that was enough, the shoe section was next. It was dark at night until I was still figuring all these things out as these so-called possessions were all over the place: pens, diaries, stationery, smartphone covers, chargers, gadgets, etc. It was midnight and I was tired, with this stuff all over the place, I just crashed on the couch and turned on YouTube and searched, "How to deal with clutter." I saw a video on minimalism, I clicked on it, and little did I know that my life is going to be changed forever. I went through a few videos on the same topic, then I moved from TV to my laptop and started reading articles, research papers, and blogs on minimalism. The topic was so interesting that I kept reading until morning. Since then, I practice minimalism, and I cannot express in words what a blessing it is to be a minimalist.

Living with less has resurfaced in today's world where most purchases are purposeless and impulsive. What happened to the stuff I had back then? Well, I kept very little to survive for the next six months and gave away everything else to the poor and needy. Of course, I felt bad while it was being taken away, but after seeing those empty closets and hanging spaces, I felt like somebody has paid off my debt beyond my knowledge. And there is no exaggeration.

Let's try something quick. Imagine you are referring to a video recipe and cooking something. Now, something on the pan is about to get burnt, and you have very little time to handle it. You quickly reach out to the kitchen drawer while looking at the pan because you can't take your eyes off it. Your hands are trying to reach out for the spatula, but all you can find are spoons, forks, a garlic peeler, an avocado slicer, and whatnot (except the spatula). Finally, your million-dollar dish is burnt, and it goes straight to the bin. Has this not happened before in some form or another? Maybe not with the kitchen drawer, but with your closet when you want to wear a particular piece of clothing or when you can't find your favourite cosmetic or perfume. We have all been through it, and it's time to declutter.

So, you're ready to dive into the world of minimalism? Step one: Marie Kondo your entire life. Bid farewell to that collection of souvenir shot glasses from every vacation you've ever taken (who needs reminders of Cancun '99 anyway?). Step two: downsize your living space. Tiny house, tiny problems, right? Step three: simplify your social calendar—sorry, can't have kids or take vacations, and definitely no room for a car in your minimalist utopia!

But before you start panicking about abandoning all your dreams and living in a tent in the woods, or to close this book forever, take a deep breath. I'm kidding. Here's the scoop: minimalism isn't about living in a sterile white room with only a toothbrush and a pair of socks. It's about intentional living, focusing on what truly brings you joy, and letting go of the excess clutter—both physical and mental. So, embrace the process of decluttering and simplifying your life, but remember, life is meant to be lived, not meticulously curated into a Pinterest board.

Now, go ahead, chuckle at your collection of novelty hats and bid adieu to that dusty treadmill doubling as a coat rack. Minimalism isn't about deprivation; it's about liberation from the stuff that weighs you down. So, declutter with a smile, embrace the quirky journey, and remember, you can still have kids, take vacations, and buy a car. Just maybe not all at once, and maybe not in neon pink.

Minimalism is a lifestyle and design philosophy based on the idea of simplicity and intentionality in every aspect of life. It involves reducing excess and focusing on what truly matters, whether in terms of possessions, activities, or thoughts. The goal of minimalism is to eliminate the unnecessary, to make room for the meaningful, thus enhancing one's quality of life and fostering a sense of clarity and purpose.

The roots of minimalism can be traced back to various cultural, religious, and philosophical traditions as well. In Western history, minimalism in art and design emerged prominently in the mid-20th century as a reaction against the excesses of abstract expressionism. Beyond the arts, minimalism has deep philosophical and spiritual antecedents. Stoicism, a philosophy that originated in ancient Greece, advocated for self-control, rationality, and the rejection of unnecessary desires. Similarly, various Eastern philosophies and religions, such as Buddhism and Zen, emphasise simplicity, mindfulness, and detachment from material possessions as paths to enlightenment and inner peace.

In contemporary society, minimalism has gained renewed popularity as a response to the pervasive consumerism and materialism of modern life. Influential figures such as Marie Kondo, with her "KonMari" method of decluttering, and the authors of "The Minimalists," Joshua Fields Millburn and Ryan Nicodemus, have popularised the idea of living with less to achieve more meaningful and fulfilling lives. Minimalism encourages individuals to critically evaluate their belongings and habits, discarding what does not add value or joy.

Adopting a minimalist lifestyle can lead to numerous benefits, including reduced stress, increased financial savings, and a greater focus on personal relationships and experiences. By intentionally simplifying their surroundings and routines, individuals can cultivate a sense of freedom and mental clarity, allowing them to pursue their true passions and goals without the distractions of excess. In essence, minimalism is about creating space—both physical and mental—for what truly matters, enabling a life of purpose and intentionality.

Minimalism offers a multitude of benefits that can significantly enhance the quality of your life. By embracing a minimalist lifestyle, individuals can experience reduced stress and anxiety as they declutter their physical and mental spaces. The act of simplifying and organising one's environment can lead to a sense of order and calm, making it easier to focus on what truly matters. Financial benefits are also prominent, as minimalism encourages mindful spending and a conscious approach to consumerism. By prioritising necessities and meaningful purchases over impulsive buys, individuals can save money and reduce financial strain.

Moreover, minimalism fosters greater clarity and purpose. By eliminating distractions and extraneous possessions, people can home in on their values, passions, and goals. This intentional focus can lead to more meaningful relationships and experiences, as minimalists often prioritise connections and activities that align with their core values. The reduced emphasis on material possessions can also promote sustainability and environmental responsibility, as minimalists typically consume less and generate less waste.

Another significant benefit of minimalism is the cultivation of mental and emotional well-being. The process of letting go of excess can be liberating, providing a sense of freedom and control over one's life. Minimalism encourages mindfulness and presence, helping individuals appreciate the present-moment and find joy in simplicity. This shift in perspective can lead to increased contentment and happiness, as people learn to value experiences and relationships over material wealth.

In essence, minimalism is not just about having fewer things, but about making room for more of what truly enriches life. By focusing on what is essential and letting go of the rest, individuals can create a more intentional, fulfilling, and balanced life.

Practicing minimalism in today's chaotic world requires intentionality, mindfulness, and a commitment to simplifying various aspects of life. Here are some practical steps to help you embrace minimalism:

Declutter Your Space: Start by decluttering your living and working environments. Go through your belongings and identify items that are essential and bring you joy. Donate, sell, or recycle items that no longer serve a purpose or contribute to your well-being. Aim to keep only those things that add value to your life. I follow a few simple steps; I keep a box in the house with a date on it. Whenever I come across any household item or a piece of clothing that I'm not sure about, I keep it in that box. I revisit the box every three months. If I never used anything from that box, I give the entire box away.

Simplify Your Schedule: Evaluate your daily and weekly routines to identify activities and people that drain your time and energy without providing significant benefits. Prioritise commitments that align with your values and goals, and learn to say no to obligations that do not. Create a balanced schedule that allows for downtime and reflection.

Mindful Consumption: Adopt a mindful approach to purchasing new items. Before buying something, ask yourself if it is necessary, if it will add value to your life, and if it aligns with your long-term goals. Avoid impulsive shopping and focus on quality over quantity. This approach not only saves money but also reduces clutter. Give it a thought, despite enticing discounts at stores or malls, they may tempt you to fill your wardrobe unnecessarily while emptying your pockets, without truly fulfilling your needs. End-of-season sale or discounted ticket prices won't increase your needs.

Digital Minimalism: In a world dominated by digital noise, practicing digital minimalism can significantly enhance your mental clarity and focus. Limit screen time, unsubscribe from unnecessary email lists or programmes, and organise your digital files. Curate your social media feeds to include only content that inspires and uplifts you (@minimalauthorspeaks is a good one ☺), and take regular breaks from technology to reconnect with the physical world.

Cultivate Mindfulness: Incorporate mindfulness practices such as meditation, deep breathing, or journaling into your daily routine. Mindfulness helps you stay present, appreciate the moment, and make intentional choices, rather than reacting to external pressures. This mental clarity is essential for maintaining a minimalist lifestyle.

Focus on Experiences: Shift your focus from accumulating material possessions to creating meaningful experiences. Invest in activities that bring you joy, foster personal growth, and strengthen relationships. Experiences often provide lasting happiness and memories, unlike material goods that can quickly lose their appeal.

Set Clear Goals: Define your personal and financial goals clearly. Knowing what you want to achieve helps you prioritise your resources and efforts towards what truly matters. Regularly review and adjust your goals to ensure they remain aligned with your values and aspirations.

Create a Supportive Environment: Surround yourself with people who understand and support your minimalist journey. Engage in communities, both online and offline, that share minimalist values and can offer encouragement and practical advice. Sharing your experiences and challenges with like-minded individuals can provide motivation and accountability.

By adopting these practices, you can navigate today's chaotic world with a minimalist mindset, reducing stress and distractions while enhancing your overall quality of life. Minimalism is a continuous journey of intentional living, helping you focus on what truly matters and fostering a sense of peace and fulfilment.

THE DEAD DIET

In a bustling city not unlike any other, lived a man named Marcus. He was an ordinary person, consumed by the daily grind of work, errands, and the elusive search for convenience. Little did Marcus know, the choices he made every day were leading him down a path of silent destruction.

One morning, Marcus awoke to the sound of his alarm blaring. He groggily made his way to the kitchen and reached for his usual breakfast: a bowl of sugary cereal and a cup of instant coffee. He didn't have time to think about nutrition; he just needed to fuel up and get to work.

As he drove to his office, Marcus noticed a new billboard towering above the freeway. It advertised a brand-new fast-food burger, "The Ultimate Feast." The sight of the juicy burger with layers of cheese, bacon, and a special sauce made his mouth water. Without a second thought, he decided to treat himself to this enticing meal for lunch.

The day at work was long and stressful. By noon, Marcus was more than ready for his indulgent lunch. He ordered the Ultimate Feast combo, complete with a side of fries and a large soda. As he bit into the burger, a surge of pleasure rushed through him. The flavours were sensational, but they masked a hidden truth.

Weeks turned into months, and Marcus fell into a routine of convenience. Breakfast was always sugary and processed, lunch was often fast-food, and dinner was usually something quick and microwavable. His energy levels started to dip, and he found himself feeling sluggish and bloated. Yet, the allure of the convenience and taste kept him trapped.

One day, Marcus started experiencing unusual symptoms. He felt constantly tired, thirsty, and noticed that he was losing weight despite his unhealthy diet. His frequent trips to the bathroom became increasingly concerning. Ignoring these signs, he continued his lifestyle, thinking it was just stress or a temporary phase.

Finally, after a particularly bad bout of dizziness at work, his colleague urged him to see a doctor. Reluctantly, Marcus made an appointment. The doctor ran several tests and called Marcus back for the results.

"Marcus, I'm afraid you have Type 2 diabetes," the doctor said gently. "Your blood sugar levels are dangerously high. This is a wake-up call. Your diet and lifestyle need a serious overhaul."

The diagnosis hit Marcus like a tonne of bricks. He was in shock and disbelief. How could this happen to him? He had always thought he was invincible, immune to the consequences of his daily choices.

Leaving the doctor's office, Marcus felt a mix of fear and determination. He realised that his diet of convenience and pleasure had led him to this point. The sugary cereal, the fast-food, the processed dinners – they were all part of the hidden feast of horrors that had been slowly eroding his health.

That evening, he sat at his kitchen table, surrounded by the remnants of his old habits. The cereal box, the empty fast-food wrappers, and the microwavable meal packages seemed to mock him. With a deep breath, Marcus made a decision. This diagnosis was his wake-up call, and he was going to change.

He began by educating himself about nutrition. He swapped his sugary cereal for oatmeal topped with fresh fruits and nuts. Lunches became colourful salads with lean proteins, and dinners were homemade, filled with vegetables and whole grains. He started exercising regularly, initially with short walks that gradually turned into longer, more vigorous activities.

As weeks turned into months, Marcus noticed remarkable changes. His energy levels soared, his mind felt clearer, and his overall mood improved. The bloating and sluggishness were replaced by a sense of vitality he hadn't felt in years. Regular check-ups showed his blood sugar levels were improving, and he was on the path to managing his diabetes effectively.

Marcus shared his story with friends and colleagues, encouraging them to look beyond the facade of convenience and taste. Together, they embarked on a journey to reclaim their health, one mindful meal at a time.

In the end, Marcus learned that the horrors of his daily diet were not just about the food itself, but the disconnection from what truly nourished his body and soul. By choosing wisely and prioritising real, wholesome foods, he transformed his life and inspired others to do the same.

And so, the hidden feast of horrors was replaced by a celebration of health and vitality, proving that with awareness and determination, anyone could break free from the chains of convenience and embrace the true essence of nourishment.

Though I have fictionalised the above story, please ask yourself, are you not able to relate to Marcus, especially my corporate world folks, signed up for a race they are completely unaware of. Funny part about this rat race is that it never ends; you end up your health, happiness, and peace of mind. The race goes on, with or without you. Like Marcus, you too must be thinking that you are eating healthy or nutritious, but is that real, let's find out.

Please look at this image below. I have taken this image, and a lot in my life has changed since I started reading the food labels. Take a look at the image below, and before reading further, try to understand the point I want to make.

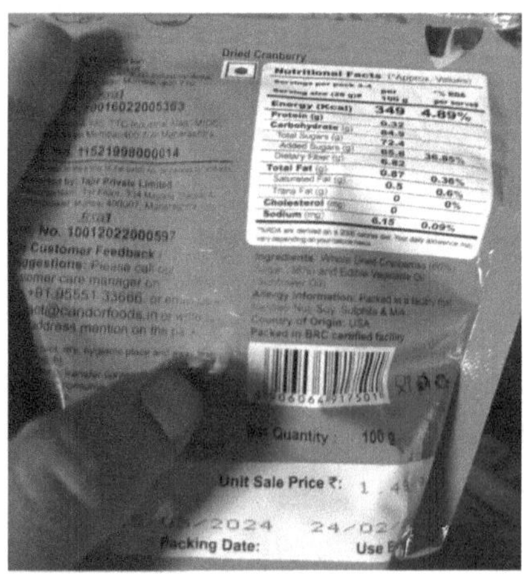

I bought this packet from a supermarket because they were marketed as dried cranberries. If you take a closer look, this "healthy" looking snack contains sugar, 38% to be precise, and vegetable oil. What the beep is wrong with our world? Nature is giving us such gems, and we are destroying them in such a way? The above is just a small example of how we are being fooled by food labels and misleading advertisements. And it is not difficult at all to come out of all these traps. Meal replacement shakes, fad diets, highly processed foods, a variety of supplements, gut cleansing pills or powders, and the packet culture are killing us. I remember a quote from a famous gastroenterologist; he says, "when you are tearing a packet of food, you are actually tearing a piece of your liver." Sounds scary, right? Well, we are just getting started. Let's take a deep dive into a simple term which is the most talked about, written about, and over-complicated these days.

Hunger

Hunger is a basic biological signal that tells us when our bodies need energy. It's controlled by the hypothalamus in the brain, which responds to hormones like ghrelin from the stomach, making us feel hungry, and leptin from fat cells, making us feel full.

Today, the simplicity of hunger is often over-complicated. Diet trends, emotional eating, abundant food availability, and technology all create confusion about when and what to eat. However, at its core, hunger is a straightforward process: our bodies signal when we need food, and we eat to satisfy that need.

By paying attention to these natural signals and avoiding external influences, we can maintain a healthy and intuitive relationship with food. Let's further dive into two types of hunger that you never knew exist, but you may be a slave to:

Hunger is not a one-dimensional experience; it can manifest in both physical and psychological forms. Understanding the distinction between physical hunger and mental hunger is essential for developing a healthy relationship with food.

Physical Hunger: This is the physiological sensation of needing food, driven by the body's requirement for energy and nutrients. It is regulated by the hypothalamus in response to hormones like ghrelin (which signals hunger) and leptin (which signals fullness). Physical hunger can be recognised by physical cues such as a growling stomach, low energy levels, and difficulty concentrating. It typically develops gradually and can be satisfied by eating a balanced meal, some fruit, or a snack.

Emotional Hunger: Unlike physical hunger, emotional hunger is not driven by physical needs. Instead, it is influenced by psychological factors such as emotions, stress, boredom, or cravings. Mental hunger often arises suddenly and can lead to specific food cravings, such as wanting sweets or comfort foods, even when the body does not need additional energy. This type of hunger is more about the mind seeking pleasure or distraction, rather than the body needing sustenance.

Understanding the difference between these two types of hunger can help individuals make more mindful eating choices. When you feel hungry, take a moment to assess whether the sensation is coming from a genuine physical need or from an emotional or mental state. Responding appropriately to physical hunger with nourishing foods and addressing mental hunger through other means, like engaging in a hobby or practicing relaxation techniques, can promote better overall health and well-being.

"You know what, Chris Hemsworth eats six meals in a day, look at him. From tomorrow I'm going to follow his diet plan." I heard somebody saying it, and I felt very sorry for that person. Just because you have information, you just don't have to follow it blindly. He is a movie star, you are an engineer or somebody working on a laptop, where are all these six meal theories coming from? Half of your problems will be solved if you understand one simple thing, "Although the human population has crossed eight billion, each human body is different. You are different too and so is your fingerprint and so is your gut bacteria." Do yourself and your health a favour and stop all this. Nutrition, hunger, and the human body are not so complicated. If you don't want to read or don't have time for it, just observe or remember how people lived and ate a few decades ago, just take a look at your grandparents and their eating habits and learn. Food and nutrition are surrounded by a galaxy of myths. Let's boldly go where few have gone before and uncover the truth behind these popular misconceptions. Now that we have come so far, let's bust some common myths about our foods today. Get ready to have your mind and taste buds tantalised.

Debunking Food Myths: A Tasty Truth Expedition

Myth 1: Carbs are the Enemy

You might have heard the whispers in the dark corners of the diet world: "Carbs will make you fat!" Let's shed some light here. Carbohydrates are your body's preferred energy source, especially for your brain and muscles. Complex carbs like whole grains, fruits, and veggies are packed with fibre, vitamins, and minerals. So, don't demonise the dough - just opt for whole grain instead of white bread.

Myth 2: Eating Fat Makes You Fat

Hold onto your avocados because this myth is about to be busted wide open. Not all fats are created equal. Healthy fats, like those found in olive oil and nuts, are essential for brain health, hormone production, and absorbing fat-soluble vitamins. It's the trans fats and excessive saturated fats that you need to watch out for. So, go ahead and enjoy that guacamole - your brain will thank you!

Myth 3: Detox Diets are Necessary

Feeling sluggish? Bloated? Enter the detox diet, promising to cleanse your body of toxins. But here's the truth: your liver and kidneys are already doing an excellent job of detoxing. Those fancy juice cleanses and detox teas? They might lighten your wallet more than your toxin load. Stick to a balanced diet with plenty of water and let your organs do their thing.

Myth 4: Gluten-Free is Healthier for Everyone

Unless you have celiac disease or a gluten sensitivity, there's no need to fear the gluten monster. Gluten-free doesn't automatically mean healthier – many gluten-free products are heavily processed and can lack essential nutrients. So, unless gluten is genuinely your nemesis, enjoy that whole-grain bread guilt-free.

Myth 5: You Should Avoid Eating at Night

The clock strikes 8 PM, and you eye that leftover pizza with guilt. But wait – it's not the hour that matters, it's the calorie count and your overall diet. Eating late doesn't inherently cause weight gain. Just be mindful of portion sizes and avoid mindless munching in front of the TV. That midnight snack might not be the villain after all.

Myth 6: All Calories are Created Equal

Sure, a calorie is a calorie in terms of energy. But nutritionally? It's a different story. 200 calories of broccoli provide fibre, vitamins, and minerals, whereas 200 calories of candy bring sugar and little else. Focus on nutrient-dense foods to fuel your body, not just calorie count.

Myth 7: You Must Drink Eight Glasses of Water a Day

Hydration is crucial, but there's no magic number. Your water needs depend on various factors like your activity level, climate, and diet. Listen to your body – if you're thirsty, drink. And remember, foods with high water content (like cucumbers and oranges) contribute to your hydration, too.

Myth 8: Supplements Can Replace a Balanced Diet

Popping a multivitamin in the morning doesn't give you a free pass to eat junk all day. Supplements are meant to fill gaps, not replace whole foods. A balanced diet full of fruits, vegetables, lean proteins, and whole grains is the best way to ensure you get the nutrients you need.

Final Bite

Food myths can be as sticky as a caramel apple, but armed with the truth, you can make healthier choices. Embrace carbs, fats, and the occasional late-night snack. Skip the detox fads and gluten-free hype unless medically necessary. If you have a goal in mind or need help to lose or gain weight, seek professional help. You have only one body, don't use it for an experiment that may cause you harm. Focus on a balanced, nutrient-rich diet, and your body will thank you. Bon appétit to a healthier you!

EXERCISE | HUSTLE FOR MUSCLE

In today's whirlwind of a world, where the demands of work, family, and endless to-do lists consume our every waking moment, finding time for exercise can feel like an insurmountable challenge. Yet, amidst the chaos, the importance of exercise has never been more crucial. Exercise is the cornerstone of maintaining our physical health, but its benefits extend far beyond the surface. It is a powerful antidote to the stress and anxiety that modern life relentlessly heaps upon us. Picture the sensation of lacing up your sneakers for a brisk morning walk, the sun casting a golden hue over your path, the cool air filling your lungs, and the rhythmic crunch of leaves underfoot grounding you in the present-moment. When was the last time you witnessed it?

Imagine the invigorating rush of endorphins flooding your system after a satisfying run, the weight of the day's worries lifting off your shoulders with every step. Envision the quiet satisfaction of completing a yoga session, your muscles stretching and releasing tension you didn't even realise you were holding onto. Exercise is not just about chiselling the perfect physique or running marathons; it's about reclaiming a piece of tranquillity in our hectic lives.

In the midst of conference calls, school pickups, and household chores, exercise carves out a sacred space for self-care. It's the solace of a quiet yoga session in the corner of a bustling gym, the laughter shared during a dance class with friends, and the sense of accomplishment as you push through that last rep at the end of a challenging workout. Exercise weaves itself into the fabric of our daily routines, offering not only physical benefits but also a profound sense of mental clarity and emotional balance.

Think of the times you've felt drained by the demands of the day, only to find a renewed sense of energy and focus after a workout. It's during these moments that exercise reveals its true power: it reminds us to pause, breathe, and reconnect with ourselves. It provides a sanctuary where we can recharge, where the noise of the outside world fades away, leaving us with a sense of calm and resilience.

In a world that often feels like it's moving at breakneck speed, exercise is the steady, grounding force that helps us navigate the whirlwind. It equips us with the strength to meet our challenges head-on, the stamina to keep up with our busy schedules, and the clarity to make thoughtful decisions. In every drop of sweat and every beat of our hearts, exercise echoes the message that amidst the hustle and bustle, we must take care of ourselves, for it is in our own well-being that we find the strength to care for everything and everyone else.

WHY YOU DON'T EXERCISE

Do you really want to hear from me? Okay, let's be brutally honest: it's not just about lack of time or motivation. It's the exhaustion that settles in after a long day, when the thought of hitting the gym feels like an additional burden rather than a relief. Picture this: you finally get home after battling through traffic or a hectic day at work, and the last thing you want to do is change into workout clothes and push yourself further. It's easier to collapse on the couch, craving relaxation and a moment to decompress.

Then there's the constant buzz of responsibilities that tether us to our daily routines. Emails flood our inboxes, deadlines loom, and family obligations pull us in multiple directions. We tell ourselves we'll exercise after we finish that last task or respond to that urgent message, but the day slips away, and so does our motivation.

There's also the allure of comfort and convenience. It's tempting to choose the couch and a favourite TV show over the discomfort of breaking a sweat or the effort required to plan and prepare a healthy meal. Fast-food beckons with its ease and familiarity, offering a quick-fix to hunger pangs, without the guilt of spending more time in the kitchen.

Let's not forget the mental barriers we erect, often unknowingly. Fear of failure whispers in our minds, urging us to avoid the embarrassment of not knowing how to use gym equipment or feeling out of place in a fitness class. It's easier to stay within our comfort zones, where familiarity shields us from the discomfort of trying something new or pushing our physical limits.

And then there's guilt, a pervasive emotion that sneaks in when we consider taking time for ourselves. We prioritise the needs of others - our families, friends, and colleagues - often at the expense of our own well-being. The thought of dedicating an hour to exercise can feel selfish when there are so many demands on our time and attention.

In truth, the barriers to exercise are as much psychological and emotional as they are physical. Overcoming them requires not just a change in routine but a shift in mindset, a recognition that prioritising our health isn't selfish but essential for our overall well-being. It's about carving out time, finding activities that bring joy and fulfilment, and understanding that self-care is not a luxury but a necessity in navigating life's challenges with resilience and vitality.

We hide behind the excuse of busyness, but often it's fear of discomfort, fear of starting, and fear of failing that holds us back. It's easier to stay in our comfort zone, but in doing so, we sacrifice our well-being. Think about the countless times you've resolved to start a new fitness routine, only to be daunted by the soreness of the first workout. The comfort of familiarity pulls us back into our old habits.

We know all this, yet we continue the cycle, hoping for a break that never comes unless we make it ourselves. Deep down, we understand that these reasons, while valid, are obstacles we have the power to overcome. It requires discipline, a shift in mindset, a commitment to prioritise our health, and the courage to step out of our comfort zones. Only then can we break free from the excuses and embrace the benefits that regular exercise brings to our lives.

WHY YOU SHOULD EXERCISE

Exercise is often touted for its obvious benefits like weight loss and muscle gain, but its impact reaches far deeper into our overall well-being, offering surprising perks that many overlook. For starters, there's the sheer, almost heavenly feeling of sweat leaving your body during a rigorous workout. It's as if the physical exertion is not just burning calories but also flushing out the stresses and toxins accumulated from daily life. This process is a natural detox, leaving you feeling lighter and rejuvenated. Then, there's the incredible rush of endorphins, the body's natural painkillers and mood elevators. These "feel-good" hormones create a state of euphoria, often referred to as a "runner's high," which can be more effective than some forms of therapy for combating depression and anxiety.

Beyond the immediate rush of endorphins, regular exercise stimulates the production of dopamine, the neurotransmitter responsible for pleasure and reward. Increased dopamine levels can enhance motivation, focus, and overall cognitive function, making you not just happier but also more productive and mentally sharp. Additionally, exercise promotes neurogenesis, the creation of new brain cells, which improves memory and cognitive abilities, potentially warding off age-related cognitive decline and diseases like Alzheimer's.

Furthermore, engaging in physical activity can enhance your immune system. Regular, moderate exercise increases the circulation of immune cells in the body, making it more efficient at identifying and combating infections. This means fewer colds and illnesses, allowing you to stay healthier throughout the year.

On a more cellular level, exercise has been shown to slow down the ageing process. It protects telomeres, the tiny caps at the end of our DNA strands, which naturally shorten with age. By preserving telomere length, exercise helps maintain the integrity of our genetic information, leading to longer, healthier lifespans.

Finally, let's not overlook the often underestimated benefit of improved sleep. Physical activity increases the amount of deep sleep you get, which is crucial for the body's recovery and repair processes. Better sleep quality translates to better overall health, more energy during the day, and an improved mood.

In essence, exercise is a powerful, multifaceted tool that enriches our lives in surprising and profound ways, far beyond the aesthetic and superficial benefits most commonly associated with it. It's a holistic enhancer of mind, body, and spirit, offering rewards that ripple through every aspect of our lives.

When we exercise or work out, our bodies undergo a complex and dynamic process that involves the release and regulation of various hormones. These hormones play crucial roles in enhancing our performance, facilitating recovery, and promoting overall well-being. Understanding how these hormones interact during physical activity can provide valuable insights into the profound effects exercise has on our bodies and minds. In the following paragraphs, we will explore the key hormones that are released or regulated during exercise and their specific functions.

Endorphins

Often referred to as the body's natural painkillers, endorphins are released during prolonged physical activity. These hormones interact with receptors in the brain to reduce the perception of pain and trigger a positive feeling in the body, similar to that of morphine. Endorphins are responsible for the "runner's high" that many athletes experience, providing a sense of euphoria and well-being that can help alleviate stress and improve mood.

Dopamine

Exercise can stimulate the production of dopamine, a neurotransmitter that plays a significant role in the brain's reward and pleasure centres. Increased levels of dopamine during physical activity can enhance motivation, improve mood, and boost feelings of pleasure and satisfaction. This hormone is essential for maintaining motivation and focus, helping individuals stick to their exercise routines and enjoy the process.

Serotonin

Known as the "feel-good" hormone, serotonin is another neurotransmitter that is influenced by physical activity. Exercise increases the availability of tryptophan, an amino acid that the brain uses to produce serotonin. Higher levels of serotonin can lead to improved mood, reduced anxiety, and a greater sense of well-being. This hormone also plays a role in regulating sleep, appetite, and digestion, contributing to overall health.

Norepinephrine

Physical activity stimulates the release of norepinephrine, a hormone and neurotransmitter that enhances alertness, concentration, and energy. It prepares the body for action by increasing heart rate, blood pressure, and blood flow to muscles. Norepinephrine helps the body respond to the demands of exercise, improving focus and performance, while also helping to manage stress more effectively.

Adrenaline (Epinephrine)

Released from the adrenal glands during exercise, adrenaline boosts the body's fight-or-flight response. It increases heart rate, dilates air passages, and mobilises energy stores, providing a surge of energy and enhancing physical performance. Adrenaline helps to increase stamina and endurance, allowing individuals to push harder and achieve better results during their workouts.

Brain-Derived Neurotrophic Factor (BDNF)

Exercise stimulates the production of BDNF, a protein that supports the survival, growth, and differentiation of neurons in the brain. BDNF plays a crucial role in brain health, enhancing cognitive function, memory, and learning. Higher levels of BDNF are associated with improved mental clarity and a reduced risk of neurodegenerative diseases, making it a vital component of the exercise-induced brain benefits.

Endocannabinoids: These naturally occurring compounds, similar to the active ingredients in cannabis, are released during exercise and contribute to the sensation of a "runner's high." Endocannabinoids bind to cannabinoid receptors in the brain, promoting feelings of euphoria, relaxation, and pain relief. They play a role in regulating mood, appetite, and memory, enhancing the overall positive effects of physical activity.

Each of these hormones contributes uniquely to the benefits of exercise, working together to enhance physical performance, improve mental health, and promote overall well-being. By understanding the hormonal responses to exercise, we can better appreciate the profound impact that regular physical activity has on our bodies and minds.

You must be wondering, "Fine, we know exercise is important, but gyms are expensive, and we don't have the time and money to travel to a gym and workout." Well, what if I tell you that we all can attain the same level of fitness without all the hustle? Maintaining physical fitness is more accessible than you might think. Contrary to popular belief, achieving a healthy and fit body doesn't require a fancy gym membership or expensive equipment. Exercising at home offers a flexible, convenient, and cost-effective alternative that can easily fit into your busy schedule. Whether you're a beginner or a seasoned fitness enthusiast, your home can become your personal gym with a bit of creativity and commitment. From body-weight exercises and simple household items to a plethora of online resources and fitness apps, you have all the tools you need at your fingertips. In this section, we will explore the myriad ways to create an effective home workout routine, demonstrating that you can achieve your fitness goals without ever stepping foot in a gym. Embrace the comfort and convenience of your own space, and discover how easy and enjoyable staying active can be right where you are. Let's dive into it:

Stretching

Starting your home workout with stretching is essential for preparing your body and mind for physical activity. Stretching improves flexibility, reduces the risk of injury, and enhances blood flow to your muscles. Simple routines like reaching for your toes, side bends, and arm circles can loosen up tight areas and increase your range of motion. Incorporating a few minutes of stretching before and after your workout can make a significant difference in your overall fitness experience.

Pro Tip: Stretching before bed can help relax muscles, release tension, and promote better sleep quality for many people, although its effectiveness and suitability can vary depending on your preferences and physical conditions.

Walking

Walking is a highly underrated, yet effective form of exercise that you can easily incorporate into your home routine. Whether you have a treadmill or simply walk around your living space or yard, walking can help improve cardiovascular health, strengthen your muscles, and boost your mood. Aim for brisk walking to get your heart rate up and enjoy the numerous health benefits it offers, all without needing any special equipment.

Jogging

If you're looking to take your cardio workout up a notch, jogging is a fantastic option. Even if space is limited, jogging in place or around a small area can elevate your heart rate, burn calories, and enhance your endurance.

It's a great way to get your blood pumping and release endorphins, those feel-good hormones that can help reduce stress and improve your overall sense of well-being.

Push-Ups

Push-ups are a fundamental body-weight exercise that effectively strengthen your upper body and core. By engaging your chest, shoulders, triceps, and abdominal muscles, push-ups help build overall upper body strength and stability. They can be performed anywhere with minimal space, and variations such as knee push-ups or incline push-ups can accommodate different fitness levels. Incorporating push-ups into your home workout routine can lead to noticeable improvements in muscle tone and endurance.

Pull-Ups

Pull-ups are a challenging yet rewarding exercise that primarily targets your back, shoulders, and arms. Using a sturdy bar or even a door frame pull-up bar, you can perform this exercise at home to develop significant upper body strength. Pull-ups require you to lift your entire body-weight, making them highly effective for building muscle and enhancing functional fitness. If you're a beginner, assisted pull-ups or negative pull-ups can help you build the necessary strength over time.

Squats

Squats are a powerhouse exercise for your lower body, engaging your thighs, hips, and glutes. This compound movement is excellent for building muscle, improving balance, and enhancing overall lower body strength. You can perform squats with just your body-weight or add intensity by holding weights like dumbbells or household items. Regularly incorporating squats into your home workouts can lead to stronger legs and better overall functional fitness, supporting daily activities with ease.

Planks

Planks are an isometric core exercise that strengthens your entire body by engaging your abdominal muscles, back, and shoulders. Holding a plank position helps improve core stability, posture, and endurance. Variations, such as side planks or planks with shoulder taps, can add variety and challenge to your routine. Planks require no equipment and can be performed in a small space, making them an ideal addition to any home workout regimen.

Skipping

Skipping, or jumping rope, is a fun and effective cardiovascular exercise that can be done in a small space. It boosts your heart health, burns calories, and improves coordination and agility. Plus, it's an activity that can easily be adjusted for intensity, making it suitable for beginners and advanced fitness enthusiasts alike. Just a few minutes of skipping can provide a high-intensity workout that energises your body and mind.

Yoga

Yoga is a holistic practice that combines physical postures, breathing exercises, and meditation to promote overall well-being. Practicing yoga at home can improve your flexibility, strength, balance, and mental clarity. With numerous online classes and tutorials available, you can find routines that suit your level and needs. Yoga not only enhances your physical health but also provides a much-needed mental break, helping you find calm and focus amidst the chaos of daily life.

Deep Breathing

Deep breathing exercises are a simple yet powerful way to enhance your mental and physical well-being. By focusing on slow, deep breaths, you can reduce stress, lower blood pressure, and improve lung capacity. Techniques such as diaphragmatic breathing or box breathing can be practiced anywhere and anytime, offering a quick way to centre yourself and promote relaxation. Integrating deep breathing exercises into your daily routine can help manage stress and improve overall health, providing a sense of calm amidst the chaos.

And if you are willing to spend a few dollars, you can take it to the next level with the below equipment-based workouts, which will take up very little space:

Dumbbell Exercises: Dumbbells are incredibly versatile and can be used for a wide range of strength training exercises that target various muscle groups. With dumbbells, you can perform exercises such as bicep curls, tricep extensions, shoulder presses, chest presses, and lunges. These exercises help in building muscle mass, improving muscle endurance, and enhancing overall strength. Dumbbells also allow for a full range of motion and unilateral training, which helps in correcting muscle imbalances and improving coordination. Incorporating dumbbells into your workout routine can lead to significant improvements in muscle tone and functional strength.

Kettlebell Exercises: Kettlebells are excellent tools for both strength training and cardiovascular workouts. Exercises like kettlebell swings, goblet squats, Turkish get-ups, and kettlebell snatches provide a comprehensive workout that targets multiple muscle groups simultaneously. The unique design of kettlebells allows for dynamic movements that improve power, endurance, and stability. Kettlebell workouts are highly effective for enhancing core strength and functional fitness, as they often involve complex, multi-joint movements that mimic real-life activities. Incorporating kettlebells into your routine can help you build strength, burn fat, and increase overall athleticism.

Resistance Band Exercises: Resistance bands are portable, affordable, and highly effective for full-body workouts. With resistance bands, you can perform exercises such as banded squats, lateral band walks, chest presses, rows, and leg extensions. These exercises help in building strength, enhancing muscle tone, and improving flexibility. Resistance bands provide variable resistance, which means the tension increases as you stretch them, making your muscles work harder through the entire range of motion. They are also excellent for rehabilitation and injury prevention, as they provide a low-impact way to strengthen muscles and joints. Integrating resistance bands into your fitness regimen can add variety and challenge, leading to better overall muscle activation and growth.

In conclusion, embracing the habit of regular exercise is not just about physical transformation—it's a profound act of self-love and resilience in today's chaotic world. While we all understand the importance of staying active, the myriad of daily responsibilities and the comfort of familiar excuses often hold us back. Yet, as we've explored, achieving fitness doesn't necessitate a gym membership or costly equipment; your home is a sanctuary where you can reclaim your health and well-being. Through simple yet effective activities like stretching, walking, jogging, body-weight exercises, skipping, yoga, and deep breathing, you have the power to transform both your body and mind.

Think about the moments when you feel overwhelmed, stressed, or disconnected from yourself. Imagine if, instead of succumbing to those feelings, you took just a few minutes to move your body and focus on your breath. Each small effort you make is a step towards a healthier, more balanced you. It's not just about the physical benefits—exercise can be your anchor, a way to find clarity amidst the chaos, and reconnect with your inner strength.

Remember, the journey to fitness is deeply personal and uniquely yours. It's about making a commitment to yourself, finding joy in movement, and recognising that every small step forward is a significant victory. Think of the moments when you chose to prioritise your well-being and how empowered and alive you felt. Let those moments be your motivation.

I urge you to start today, right where you are, with whatever you have. Don't wait for the perfect moment or the perfect setup. Your home is your gym, your body is your tool, and your mind is your greatest ally. As you embark on this journey, know that each effort, no matter how small, is a testament to your strength and determination. You have the power to change your life, one step, one movement, one repetition at a time. Your future self will thank you for every bit of effort you invest in your health and happiness. So, take that first step today—embrace the journey and discover the incredible resilience and strength that lies within you.

Bonus Tip: We all start with a lot of enthusiasm and expect rapid results. For example, if you haven't exercised in 10 years, that's 3,650 days of neglect to overcome. Expecting your body to change without putting in consistent effort is delusional. Transformation is grand, and with social media, it is a fancy term, but true progress comes from believing in small steps and committing to daily improvements. Embrace the grind and celebrate each day's progress, however small. We expect to reverse the effects of an inactive and sedentary lifestyle in a few days, failing which we give up and go back to the couch. Keep this thing in mind, you did not gain weight or develop bad health conditions overnight, so don't expect them to vanish overnight. Have patience.

I follow a method while forming any habit, and I think you should follow it too. Take one empty jar, which should be transparent, and keep it in a visible sight. Every time you work out, just add one peanut or any nut or grain of your choice; on the other hand, any day you miss your workout, take a grain out. Whenever you think you have not got any results, take a look at the jar, and you'll get your answer. The jar will not only remind you of how little effort you've taken but will also make you feel accountable. I hope you are finding a jar now. 😊

HABIT HACKS: YOUR SECRET WEAPONS AGAINST CHAOS

When life spins out of control, it's easy to feel like you're caught in a whirlwind with no escape. But amid the chaos, habits can be your hidden arsenal, turning turmoil into triumph. Imagine having a set of auto-pilot routines that keep you grounded, focused, and resilient, no matter what life throws at you. These habit hacks are not just about creating order; they're about reclaiming your power, reducing decision fatigue, and building a life that can weather any storm. Ready to turn chaos into a well-oiled machine? Let's dive into the habit hacks that will become your secret weapons against the unpredictable.

Habits aren't just routines; they're the bedrock of a stable and productive life. In the face of chaos, they provide the predictability and control that are often lacking. By establishing reliable habits, you create a sense of order and calm, making it easier to navigate through life's uncertainties. These small, consistent actions can lead to significant long-term benefits, acting as a counterbalance to the unpredictability around you. Whether it's a daily exercise regimen, a morning meditation practice, or a structured work routine, habits enable you to maintain focus and composure, helping you to stay on track and achieve your goals, even when everything else seems to be falling apart. They serve as a constant in an ever-changing world, giving you the strength and resilience to face any challenge head-on.

Habits have the power to make or break you. Good habits can elevate your life, providing the discipline and consistency needed to achieve your goals. They can transform chaos into manageable segments, allowing you to thrive even in the most challenging circumstances. On the flip side, negative habits can exacerbate chaos, leading to further disarray and stress. Unproductive routines like procrastination, poor diet, or excessive screen time can compound the effects of chaos, making it harder to regain control. It's crucial to recognise that the habits you choose to cultivate will either fortify you against the storms of life or leave you vulnerable to being swept away. The right habits act as your shield, protecting your mental and physical well-being, while the wrong ones can dismantle the very foundation of stability you're trying to build.

Take a moment to introspect and reflect on your daily habits. Are you confident that your routines are contributing to your life's purpose, or are you merely running on auto-pilot, getting dragged by the currents of chaos? This is your life, your story—every habit you cultivate writes a line in it. Do your daily actions align with your values and aspirations, or do they just fill the hours? If you want to be fit for life, but you don't exercise at all and you start your day with sugary cereals and toast, that won't take you to your goal ever. It's easy to fall into patterns that feel comfortable but lead nowhere. Ask yourself, are your habits building the life you desire, or are they distractions from what truly matters? This is your chance to reclaim control, to consciously choose habits that propel you toward your goals, and to break free from the ones that hold you back. Your habits shape your destiny—make sure they are taking you where you truly want to go.

Viewing habits as powerful tools can transform how you approach each day. Habits are not just mundane routines but strategic actions that can significantly shape your life. They are the levers that, when pulled consistently, yield substantial and lasting changes. Think of each habit as a building block, a deliberate choice that contributes to the foundation of a purposeful life. By harnessing the power of well-chosen habits, you can steer your life in the direction you desire, creating order out of chaos and purpose out of routine. In the following sections, we will delve into practical tips and strategies for effective habit formation. These insights will help you cultivate habits that align with your goals and aspirations, turning them into powerful allies in your journey towards a more focused, resilient, and fulfilled life.

Starting a new habit can be challenging, but with the right strategies, it becomes manageable. Begin by setting clear, achievable goals to give you direction. Break these goals into small steps to make them less daunting. Use triggers or cues to remind you to perform your habit, like associating it with an existing routine. Consistency is crucial; aim to practice your habit at the same time each day. Tracking your progress can provide a sense of accomplishment and keep you motivated. Lastly, celebrate your small wins to reinforce your commitment and enjoy the journey of self-improvement.

Identify Triggers

Recognising the triggers that lead to your bad habits is the first step towards overcoming them. Triggers can be situations, emotions, people, or even specific times of day that prompt you to engage in a negative behaviour. Start by keeping a journal to track when and where your bad habit occurs, noting your emotional state and the circumstances surrounding it. Are you stressed, bored, or tired? Do certain places or people influence your behaviour? By pinpointing these triggers, you can develop strategies to avoid or modify them. For example, if stress is a trigger, you might find healthier ways to manage it, such as through exercise or meditation. Awareness of your triggers allows you to anticipate and plan for these moments, giving you greater control over your actions and helping you break the cycle of bad habits.

Replace Negative Habits

One of the most effective strategies for breaking bad habits is to replace them with positive ones that fulfil the same need. This substitution allows you to maintain the reward aspect of the habit while changing the behaviour itself. Start by identifying what need your bad habit is meeting. Is it stress relief, comfort, or a way to pass the time? Once you understand the underlying need, find a healthier habit that can serve the same purpose. For instance, if you tend to snack on unhealthy food when you're stressed, try replacing it with a quick walk or a few minutes of deep breathing exercises. If you find yourself mindlessly scrolling through social media out of boredom, pick up a book or engage in a hobby instead. The key is to ensure that the new habit provides a similar sense of satisfaction or relief. By consciously choosing positive alternatives, you can gradually phase out the negative habits and build a healthier, more productive routine.

Create Barriers

Creating barriers is a powerful strategy for preventing bad habits by making it more difficult to engage in them. Start by assessing your environment and identifying what makes it easy to fall into your negative behaviours. For example, if you tend to snack on junk food while watching TV, consider removing unhealthy snacks from your home or keeping them out of sight. If procrastination is an issue, create a dedicated workspace that minimises distractions, or use apps that block social media during work hours. Another effective barrier is to set specific rules for yourself, such as not using your phone during meals or designating certain times of day for focused work. By intentionally designing your environment to make bad habits harder to access, you empower yourself to make better choices and create a more supportive atmosphere for your positive habits to flourish.

Stay Mindful

Staying mindful is essential for breaking bad habits and fostering positive change. Mindfulness involves being present and fully aware of your thoughts, feelings, and actions in the moment. By practicing mindfulness, you can better recognise the triggers and patterns that lead to your negative behaviours. Start by incorporating mindfulness techniques into your daily routine, such as meditation, deep breathing, or simply taking a moment to pause before reacting to a situation. When you feel the urge to engage in a bad habit, take a step back and assess your emotions and motivations. Ask yourself why you feel compelled to act a certain way and whether it aligns with your goals. This self-awareness can help you make more intentional choices, steering you away from automatic reactions. By cultivating mindfulness, you empower yourself to break free from unhealthy patterns and create a more conscious, fulfilling life.

Practice Patience

Practicing patience is crucial when it comes to breaking bad habits and forming new ones. Change doesn't happen overnight, and setbacks are a natural part of the process. Understand that developing new habits takes time and consistent effort. Be gentle with yourself as you navigate this journey, recognising that every small step counts toward your larger goals. Celebrate your progress, no matter how minor, and don't be discouraged by occasional slip-ups. Instead, view them as learning opportunities that can help you adjust your strategies moving forward. By cultivating patience, you create a supportive mindset that fosters resilience and persistence, allowing you to stay committed to your transformation even when the path gets tough. Remember, lasting change is a marathon, not a sprint, and patience is your ally in achieving meaningful progress.

Starting a new habit can be challenging, but with the right strategies, it becomes manageable. Begin by setting clear, achievable goals to give you direction. Break these goals into small steps to make them less daunting. Use triggers or cues to remind you to perform your habit, like associating it with an existing routine. Consistency is crucial; aim to practice your habit at the same time each day. Tracking your progress can provide a sense of accomplishment and keep you motivated. Lastly, celebrate your small wins to reinforce your commitment and enjoy the journey of self-improvement.

MEDITATION | THE TRUE FREEDOM

*"Meditation is not a means to an end.
It is both the means and the end."*

- Jiddu Krishnamurti,

The power of meditation needs no introduction. Some of you might have heard of it, some of you might be aware, and some of you might be practitioners. In the chaos of modern life, finding moments of tranquillity can seem like an elusive dream. Yet, within the simplicity of meditation lies a profound tool for achieving inner peace and clarity. Meditation is not just an ancient practice; it is a timeless path to understanding the self and embracing the present-moment. By quieting the mind and centring our thoughts, we unlock a wellspring of calm and insight, allowing us to navigate the complexities of our daily existence with greater ease and purpose. The true essence of meditation is in its ability to connect us to

the now, transforming how we experience and interact with the world around us.

Meditation invites us to step away from the noise and distractions, guiding us to a space where we can observe our thoughts without judgement and cultivate a deeper awareness of our inner world. In this stillness, we find the strength to confront our fears, the wisdom to understand our emotions, and the serenity to appreciate life's simple joys. The practice of meditation is a sanctuary, a retreat from the chaos, where we can reconnect with our true selves and find balance in our lives.

As we delve deeper into the art of meditation, we learn that it is not about achieving a perfect state of mind, but about embracing each moment as it is. It teaches us patience, compassion, and resilience, helping us to let go of the past and anxieties about the future. Through regular practice, meditation becomes a powerful ally in our quest for self-improvement, offering us the tools to manage stress, enhance our focus, and foster a sense of inner peace that permeates every aspect of our lives.

The roots of meditation trace back thousands of years, weaving through the rich tapestry of ancient civilisations. In the depths of early history, meditation emerged as a sacred practice in spiritual and philosophical traditions across the globe. In ancient India, meditation was integral to Hinduism and later Buddhism, where it was practiced to achieve spiritual enlightenment and inner peace.

The sages and monks would retreat to serene natural settings, sitting in silent contemplation, focusing on their breath or a mantra to transcend the confines of the mind. Similarly, in ancient China, Taoist monks engaged in meditation to align themselves with the Tao, the natural order of the universe, employing techniques such as mindfulness and breath control.

Even in the West, early forms of meditation can be found in the contemplative practices of early Christian monks and mystics who sought divine connection through silent prayer and introspection. Across these diverse cultures, meditation was revered as a profound tool for exploring the inner self and understanding the mysteries of existence, a testament to its enduring significance through the ages.

In an age dominated by technology and rapid change, the significance of meditation has become increasingly profound. The constant bombardment of information, the pressures of work and personal life, and the relentless pace of modern society can leave us feeling overwhelmed and disconnected. Meditation offers a sanctuary from this chaos, a chance to pause and reconnect with our inner selves. In an era where mental health issues are on the rise, meditation provides a natural and effective way to manage stress, anxiety, and depression.

It helps us cultivate mindfulness, allowing us to live more fully in the present-moment, rather than being consumed by past regrets or future worries. Moreover, meditation enhances our focus and emotional resilience, equipping us to handle life's challenges with greater clarity and calmness. By incorporating meditation into our daily routines, we can find balance and harmony amid the turbulence, leading to a more fulfilling and centred life.

Now that we are aware of meditation, its importance, and its roots, let's learn some common meditation methods that you can practice in your daily lives. I'd recommend you to try all of them and discover which one suits you the most, gives you more mental peace, and makes you feel more centred.

Mindfulness Meditation

Mindfulness meditation, rooted in Buddhist traditions, involves paying deliberate attention to the present-moment without judgement. Practitioners typically sit quietly, focusing on their breath or bodily sensations, and gently bring their attention back whenever the mind wanders. This practice cultivates an awareness of thoughts, emotions, and physical sensations, promoting a greater understanding of the self. The benefits of mindfulness meditation are extensive, including reduced stress, improved emotional regulation, enhanced concentration, and a heightened sense of well-being. By fostering a non-reactive awareness, it helps individuals navigate daily challenges with greater ease and equanimity.

Loving-Kindness Meditation (Metta)

Loving-kindness meditation, also known as Metta, is a practice that involves generating feelings of compassion and love towards oneself and others. Practitioners begin by silently repeating phrases like "May I be happy, may I be healthy, may I be safe,," gradually extending these sentiments to loved ones, acquaintances, and even those with whom they have conflicts. This practice nurtures a sense of universal love and empathy. The benefits of loving-kindness meditation include increased positive emotions, reduced negative emotions, improved social connections, and a stronger sense of compassion and empathy. It encourages a more loving and accepting outlook towards oneself and others, fostering emotional resilience and interpersonal harmony.

Transcendental Meditation

Transcendental Meditation (TM) is a form of silent mantra meditation developed by Maharishi Mahesh Yogi. Practitioners sit comfortably with their eyes closed and silently repeat a specific mantra for 20 minutes twice a day. This technique aims to transcend ordinary thought processes, achieving a state of deep relaxation and heightened awareness. The benefits of Transcendental Meditation are well-documented, including reduced stress and anxiety, improved cognitive function, increased creativity, and a greater sense of inner peace. By allowing the mind to settle into a state of restful alertness, TM helps individuals experience profound relaxation and rejuvenation.

Body Scan Meditation

Body scan meditation is a practice that involves systematically focusing on different parts of the body, typically from head to toe, to develop a heightened awareness of bodily sensations. Practitioners lie down or sit comfortably and slowly bring their attention to each area of the body, noticing any sensations, tensions, or discomforts without judgement. This practice enhances the mind-body connection and promotes relaxation. The benefits of body scan meditation include reduced stress, improved sleep, decreased physical pain, and greater overall body awareness. By encouraging mindfulness of bodily experiences, it helps individuals release physical and mental tension, fostering a sense of calm and well-being.

Zen Meditation (Zazen)

Zen meditation, or Zazen, is a traditional Buddhist practice that involves seated meditation with an emphasis on observing thoughts and sensations without attachment. Practitioners typically sit in a lotus or half-lotus position, focusing on their breath and maintaining a straight posture. The goal is to remain present and observe the flow of thoughts and sensations without getting caught up in them. The benefits of Zen meditation include enhanced concentration, increased self-awareness, reduced stress, and a deeper sense of spiritual connection. By cultivating a disciplined and attentive mind, Zazen helps individuals develop inner clarity and equanimity, fostering a balanced and peaceful approach to life.

As we draw this chapter on meditation to a close, let us reflect on the profound simplicity and transformative power of this ancient practice. In a world that often feels overwhelming and disconnected, meditation offers a sanctuary of peace and a path to self-discovery. It teaches us to embrace the present-moment, to find stillness amidst the chaos, and to connect deeply with ourselves and others. The journey of meditation is not about perfection, but about practice and presence. It invites us to confront our inner landscapes with compassion and courage, unlocking the boundless potential within us. As you integrate meditation into your daily life, may you find not only relief from the stresses of the modern world but also a deeper, more enduring sense of purpose and joy. Let meditation be your guiding light, illuminating the path to a more mindful, balanced, and fulfilling existence.

Last but not the least, meditation and distraction go hand in hand. Whenever you get distracted, just divert your attention to the practice again. Remember, meditation is all about observation without judgement.

More power to a calmer you!

DISCIPLINED TO DOMINATE

*"Discipline is the bridge between
goals and accomplishment."*

– Jim Rohn

Out of the 8 billion people inhabiting our planet, a minuscule fraction wields the reins of global power and wealth. Among these are approximately 2,700 billionaires, whose financial prowess enables them to shape economies and influence policy.

Joining them are the top executives and business leaders, a group numbering in the tens of thousands, who guide the world's largest corporations and dictate market trends. Political leaders, approximately 2,000 to 4,000 strong, hold sway over national and international policies. Beyond these are influential media personalities, heads of major NGOs, top academics, and other key figures, summing up to around 50,000 to 100,000 individuals with substantial clout.

These individuals control everything from global economic shifts to technological advancements, environmental policies, and social movements. Their influence extends beyond mere wealth or official titles; they are the architects of change, capable of steering public opinion, enacting laws, and directing the flow of resources. But what is the common thread that ties this elite group together, granting them the ability to achieve such monumental feats?

The answer lies in a single, profound attribute: DISCIPLINE. Discipline is the bedrock upon which these powerful individuals build their empires. It is the unwavering commitment to their goals, the relentless pursuit of excellence, and the capacity to maintain focus amidst chaos.

Billionaires meticulously manage their investments and constantly innovate. Executives adhere to rigorous schedules and strategic planning. Politicians craft policies and navigate complex geopolitical landscapes with precision. Influencers and thought leaders dedicate themselves to honing their craft and expanding their reach.

Discipline is the engine driving their success, allowing them to accomplish what seems impossible to the average person. It enables them to rise early, work diligently, and persevere through challenges. They set clear, achievable goals and break them down into manageable tasks. They maintain a strong sense of purpose and direction, which guides their actions and decisions. Through disciplined habits, they maximise their productivity, harnessing every moment to its fullest potential.

In the grand tapestry of global influence, discipline is the thread that weaves through the lives of the most powerful and successful individuals. It is not merely about rigid routines, but about cultivating a mindset that values consistency, perseverance, and continuous improvement. By embracing discipline, they unlock the potential to shape the world, leaving an indelible mark on history. And so, for anyone seeking to harness their inner strength and achieve greatness, discipline is the key that opens the door to boundless possibilities.

Now that we understand the significance of discipline, let's explore the profound benefits it offers. Discipline is not just a tool for achieving success; it is a transformative force that can enhance every aspect of your life.

Increased Productivity: Discipline enables us to manage our time effectively, prioritise tasks, and maintain focus. By sticking to a structured routine, we can accomplish more in less time, leading to greater productivity and a sense of accomplishment.

Enhanced Mental Strength: Discipline builds resilience and mental toughness. It helps us stay committed to our goals, even when faced with obstacles and setbacks. This mental fortitude is crucial for overcoming challenges and maintaining a positive outlook.

Improved Health and Well-being: A disciplined approach to life often includes regular exercise, a balanced diet, and sufficient rest. These habits contribute to better physical health, increased energy levels, and overall well-being.

Stronger Relationships: Discipline fosters consistency and reliability, which are essential for building trust and strong relationships. By being disciplined in our commitments and communication, we can nurture healthier, and more fulfilling connections with others.

Financial Stability: Discipline in financial matters, such as budgeting, saving, and investing, leads to greater financial security and independence. It helps us make informed decisions and avoid impulsive spending, ensuring long-term financial well-being.

Personal Growth and Development: Discipline encourages continuous learning and self-improvement. By setting and achieving personal goals, we expand our knowledge, develop new skills, and grow as individuals.

Greater Sense of Control: Living a disciplined life gives us a sense of control over our destiny. It empowers us to make deliberate choices, align our actions with our values, and steer our lives in the direction we desire.

Incorporating discipline into our daily lives unlocks a multitude of benefits that extend far beyond the pursuit of success. It shapes our character, enhances our capabilities, and paves the way for a more fulfilling and purpose-driven existence. By embracing discipline, we can transform our lives and achieve our fullest potential.

Cultivating Discipline: Simple Hacks and Tricks

Let's explore some practical hacks and tricks to cultivate discipline in our daily lives without feeling overwhelmed by the term. Developing discipline doesn't have to be daunting; small, manageable steps can make a big difference.

Start Small: Begin with simple, achievable goals. This could be as easy as making your bed every morning or dedicating 10 minutes to exercise. Small wins build momentum and confidence.

Create a Routine: Establish a daily schedule that includes time for work, rest, and leisure. Consistency is key to building disciplined habits.

Set Clear Priorities: Identify your top three tasks for the day and focus on completing them first. This helps you stay organised and prevents procrastination.

Use Reminders and Alarms: Set reminders on your phone, or use a planner to keep track of your commitments and deadlines. This ensures you stay on top of your tasks.

Practice Self-Control: Learn to delay gratification by rewarding yourself after completing a task. This strengthens your ability to resist distractions and stay focused.

Limit Distractions: Create a workspace free from distractions, and set specific times for checking emails and social media. This helps maintain concentration and productivity.

Reflect and Adjust: At the end of each day, review what worked and what didn't. Adjust your strategies as needed to continually improve your discipline. Discipline does not follow the "one size fits all" approach, so mix and match what works for you.

By integrating these simple practices into your routine, you can gradually develop discipline without feeling overwhelmed. Remember, discipline is a skill that grows with practice and persistence.

You were not born to be a lazy ass. Deep within you lies the potential for greatness, waiting to be unleashed. Imagine the life you could lead if you harnessed the power of discipline. Picture waking up each day with purpose, conquering your goals, and living a life that truly fulfils you. It's time to shake off complacency, rise above excuses, and take charge of your destiny. Discipline is a foundational principle and not rocket science—don't overcomplicate it. On the other hand, discipline does not mean brutally torturing your body and your mind and eventually give up because your mind is smart enough to outsmart you and still make sure that your body is at comfort. It is designed to work that way. Better look at discipline as small, significant changes and enough time for your body and your mind to make peace with it. Embrace discipline as your guiding force and let it transform your dreams into reality. The journey won't always be easy, but every step forward is a testament to your strength and determination. Wake up, seize the day, and become the person you were always meant to be. Your extraordinary life begins now.

GRATITUDE

*"Gratitude can transform common days
into Thanksgivings, turn routine jobs into joy,
and change ordinary opportunities into blessings."*

– William Arthur Ward

When I hear the word 'Gratitude,' it often leaves me pondering where to begin discussing its importance in our daily lives. Just as we acknowledge 'Honesty is the best policy,' it's crucial to reflect on when we last expressed genuine thanks for the blessings we enjoy. Amidst our perpetual quest for more, have we paused to enumerate our reasons for gratitude? Have we simply taken a moment to appreciate the multitude of blessings bestowed upon us? Consider this: you woke up today, a gift denied to many around the world. To underscore this point, allow me to share a story.

In a small town in India, there once lived a man named Hazrat Moosa, rumoured to have regular conversations with the Almighty. One day, a wealthy man approached him with curiosity, asking, "I've heard you speak to the Almighty. Is that true?" Moosa affirmed, "Yes, indeed." The rich man then made a surprising request, "Could you please tell the Almighty to stop granting me wealth and prosperity? I have been given enough." Moosa agreed to convey the message.

On his way home, Moosa encountered a beggar in dire straits, wrapped in a single ragged cloth, visibly hungry, and frail. The beggar stopped him and pleaded, "I've heard you speak with the Almighty. Can you ask Him to provide me with something? Look at me compared to the wealthy man you spoke to earlier–I have nothing." Moosa promised to relay his message as well.

Days later, Moosa returned to town. The wealthy man eagerly asked, "Moosa, did you deliver my message to the Almighty?" Moosa replied, "Yes, I told Him you no longer wish for wealth and prosperity. In response, He suggested that if you no longer wish to receive His blessings, you should cease being thankful for what you already have." The wealthy man paused, reflecting deeply. "Moosa, I cannot stop being grateful. The Almighty has blessed me abundantly for so long; I cannot deny His generosity."

Continuing on his way, Moosa met the beggar once more, who anxiously inquired, "Did you speak to God about my plea?" Moosa assured him, "Yes, I did." The beggar eagerly asked, "What did He say?" Moosa conveyed the response, "He said, if you seek more, you should be thankful for what you already possess." The beggar reacted with frustration, "How can I be thankful? What do I have to be grateful for? This tattered cloth?" As he spoke, a sudden gust of wind whisked away the cloth, leaving the beggar with nothing.

The above story tells us the importance of gratitude in our daily lives. The gratitude prayer and practice aren't a new phenomenon; it has been there since ages. Gratitude practices have deep roots in various religious and cultural traditions, emphasising their universal importance across time and societies. Whether through ancient rituals or modern psychological techniques, the practice of gratitude continues to play a vital role in enhancing individual and collective well-being. Let's try to understand the specifics based on religions and civilisations.

Gratitude has been deeply rooted in various civilisations and religions throughout history. In early civilisations like Sumer and Mesopotamia, gratitude was shown through offerings and rituals to ensure favour from gods. In Ancient Egypt, rituals and prayers expressed gratitude to deities like Ra and Osiris for agricultural abundance and harmony in the universe. Hinduism emphasises gratitude as part of "dharma," honouring gods, ancestors, and gurus during festivals like Diwali and Pongal. Buddhism teaches gratitude through mindfulness and compassion, reflecting on interconnectedness and appreciating all aspects of life. Jainism extends gratitude to all forms of life through principles of non-violence (Ahimsa). In Judaism, daily prayers and festivals like Passover highlight gratitude for God's blessings and liberation. Christianity emphasises gratitude in biblical teachings and practices like the Eucharist, thanking God for Jesus Christ's sacrifice. Islam regards gratitude (shukr) as essential, expressed through daily prayers and Quranic teachings on blessings received from Allah.

Now that we've come so far, let's try to understand the core importance of gratitude in our daily lives.

The Core Importance of Gratitude

Gratitude, at its essence, is more than a mere expression of thankfulness; it is a profound recognition and appreciation of the positive aspects of life. This fundamental practice transcends cultural, religious, and temporal boundaries, highlighting its universal relevance and importance. The core importance of gratitude can be understood through its multifaceted impact on an individual's well-being, interpersonal relationships, and societal cohesion.

Enhancing Personal Well-Being

Gratitude has a transformative effect on an individual's mental and emotional health. By focusing on what one has rather than what is lacking, gratitude fosters a mindset of abundance. This shift in perspective can alleviate stress, reduce feelings of envy and resentment, and promote overall mental health. Scientific studies consistently demonstrate that individuals who regularly practice gratitude experience higher levels of happiness and lower levels of depression. This is because gratitude encourages a positive outlook on life, which can enhance resilience and emotional stability, enabling individuals to navigate life's challenges with greater ease and grace.

Strengthening Interpersonal Relationships

On a social level, gratitude acts as a powerful connector. Expressing gratitude can strengthen bonds between individuals, fostering a sense of trust and mutual appreciation. When people feel valued and recognised, they are more likely to engage positively with others, creating a ripple effect of kindness and cooperation. This dynamic is essential in building and maintaining healthy relationships, whether in families, friendships, or professional settings. By acknowledging the efforts and contributions of others, gratitude cultivates a supportive and nurturing environment where people feel motivated to contribute and collaborate.

Cultivating Spiritual and Philosophical Growth

Gratitude is also deeply intertwined with spiritual and philosophical growth. In many religious traditions, gratitude is seen as a pathway to deeper spiritual awareness and connection with the divine. It encourages humility and reverence for the greater forces at play in life. Philosophically, gratitude invites individuals to ponder the nature of existence and their place within the larger tapestry of life. It promotes a sense of wonder and appreciation for the complexity and beauty of the world.

In essence, the practice of gratitude is a cornerstone of a fulfilling and harmonious life. It nurtures our well-being by promoting a positive mindset, enhances interpersonal relationships through mutual appreciation, fosters societal cohesion by reinforcing communal bonds, and supports spiritual and philosophical growth by encouraging a profound appreciation for life. Embracing gratitude in daily life is a timeless and universally beneficial practice, one that has the power to transform individuals and societies alike.

Daily Habits to Cultivate Gratitude

Incorporating gratitude into daily life requires intentional practices that foster a positive mindset and deepen appreciation for the world around us. Here are some daily habits that can help cultivate a sense of gratitude:

Please note, unlike other chapters in this book, the practices outlined below are intentionally prescriptive. Cultivating gratitude benefits from structured guidance and principles to ensure meaningful and effective implementation.

1. Gratitude Journaling.

Description: Dedicate a few minutes each day to write down things you are grateful for. This can be done in the morning to set a positive tone for the day, or in the evening to reflect on the day's blessings.

Practice: Keep a notebook by your bed with a pen. Aim to list at least three specific things you are thankful for each day. Over time, this practice can shift your focus towards the positive aspects of life.

Pro Tip: I practice this every day, and mark my words, it can help you look at your blessings in a completely different way. For example, you got up today, many people didn't. Start being thankful from there.

2. Mindful Appreciation

Description: Mindfulness involves being present and fully engaged in the current moment. By pairing mindfulness with appreciation, you can enhance your awareness of the good in your life.

Practice: Take moments throughout the day to pause and appreciate your surroundings. Notice the beauty of nature, savour the taste of your food, or feel gratitude for a kind gesture from a friend. Mindful appreciation helps anchor you in the present and fosters a deeper sense of gratitude.

3. Expressing Gratitude to Others.

Description: Sharing your gratitude with others not only reinforces your own sense of thankfulness, but also strengthens your relationships.

Practice: Make it a habit to thank people in your life regularly. This could be through a heartfelt note, a quick message, or a verbal acknowledgement. Letting others know that you appreciate them can create a ripple effect of positivity.

4. Gratitude Rituals

Description: Establishing rituals that involve gratitude can embed this practice into your daily routine.

Practice: Integrate gratitude into existing routines, such as saying a gratitude prayer before meals, starting family gatherings with expressions of thanks, or ending the day with a gratitude reflection. Rituals provide structure and consistency, making gratitude a natural part of your life.

5. Positive Affirmations

Description: Positive affirmations are statements that reinforce a positive mindset and self-worth. When focused on gratitude, these affirmations can enhance your overall sense of well-being.

Practice: Begin your day with affirmations that highlight gratitude. Examples include, "I am grateful for the opportunities today will bring," or "I appreciate the people and experiences in my life." Repeating these affirmations can help internalise a grateful outlook.

6. Engaging in Acts of Kindness,

Description: Performing acts of kindness for others can foster a sense of gratitude, highlighting the interconnectedness of our lives.

Practice: Engage in small acts of kindness daily, such as helping a colleague, volunteering, or simply offering a smile to a stranger. These actions remind you of the impact you can have on others and enhance your appreciation for the kindness you receive in return.

7. Reflective Meditation.

Description: Meditation focused on gratitude helps calm the mind and deepen your awareness of the positive aspects of life.

Practice: Set aside a few minutes each day for reflective meditation. Find a quiet place, close your eyes, and take deep breaths. Reflect on what you are grateful for, allowing these thoughts to fill you with a sense of peace and contentment.

8. Keeping a Gratitude Jar

Description: A gratitude jar is a simple yet powerful tool to visually accumulate your daily expressions of thanks.

Practice: Each day, write down something you are grateful for on a small piece of paper and place it in the jar. Over time, the jar will fill with notes of gratitude, serving as a tangible reminder of the positivity in your life. During challenging times, revisiting these notes can uplift your spirits.

Incorporating these daily habits into your life can transform the way you perceive and interact with the world. By consistently practicing gratitude, you cultivate a mindset that seeks out and appreciates the positive, fostering greater happiness, resilience, and connection. These simple, yet effective habits can help you build a life imbued with gratitude and fulfilment.

In the tapestry of life, gratitude is the thread that binds us together with the profound awareness of abundance and the beauty of the human spirit. It reminds us that in every moment, no matter how challenging or joyous, there is always something to be thankful for. Let us carry this torch of gratitude forward, lighting the path with its warmth and illuminating even the darkest corners with hope and appreciation. For in embracing gratitude, we not only enrich our own lives, but sow seeds of kindness and connection that flourish endlessly, shaping a world where every heart beats to the rhythm of thankfulness.

WORDS ARE POWERFUL

"Words have energy and power,
with the ability to help, to heal, to hinder,
to hurt, to harm, to humiliate, and to humble."

– Yehuda Berg

Angela entered the house. It was darker than usual in the living room. Her husband and her son were watching an engaging movie in a theatre-like setup. "Are you guys insane? How can you stay inside with all the windows and blinds closed? I feel like I'll die of breathlessness in this house," she said angrily and moved to another room. Things moved back to normal, and the family had dinner. That night she slept, never to get up. Care to know the reason for her sudden death? BREATHLESSNESS!

Well, we often say things to express what our feelings are at any moment without understanding what could be the possible after-effects. The underlying secret that you are unaware of is that the mind doesn't understand the frustration, the anger, the joy, or the stress under which you are saying something. Your mind is programmed with the words you speak or think, irrespective of the emotions. Look around you, you will find a mixed bag of individuals, some high on achievement, some at a very weak or low point in their life, and some who have not moved an inch in the past few years. Why so much diversity? Well, it is all about the way you programme your mind. Self-talk is a big phenomenon. You often say or hear people using heavy words or sentences like "he will never change," "I think I won't be able to make it," "my boss is making my life miserable," "I can't see any future in this organisation," "my son never listens to me." As per an ancient theory, whatever you say in your house, your house says "Tathastu," meaning "so be it" in return, which means whatever you say to your house, your house blesses you to make it a reality. On the other hand, based on Hindu scriptures, Goddess Saraswati resides at the tip of your tongue; she blesses us with whatever we say….

Why manifest such negative and hurtful thoughts when, in reality, we don't want any of it? Our objective is something else, but in reality, we say something completely opposite, or worse.

I understand s#it happens, mood swings, and not all days are Sundays, and the fact that you can't be conscious all the time. But, the least we could do is use our words carefully, choose to remain silent, or even use the words to our advantage to come out of a bad situation, not to make it worse. The mind can only process words, not emotions with which they are said or situations in which they are used. More importantly, we have two kinds of conversations, one with others and one with ourselves; the latter one is more important if you want health, peace, prosperity, and growth. People with stellar achievements programme their subconscious minds every day. Making sure what you talk to yourself and what you want from life are in sync is of utmost importance. Even if I keep the top achievers aside, the most common people amongst us who wish to lead a happy and fulfilling life need to have a positive inner dialogue. I cannot emphasise enough the importance of it.

Words are often described as powerful because they influence our thoughts, mindset, beliefs, emotions, and actions. Words can evoke a range of strong emotions. Compliments, encouragement, and kind words can uplift and motivate people, while insults, raw criticism, and harsh words can demoralise and break them. The emotional impact of words can be long-lasting.

Words can have a significant impact in the work environment too. An experiment was conducted with a few professionals from a range of different skill sets and backgrounds. These professionals were equally divided into two sets and were given the same set of tasks with the same guidelines and timelines, except one group had a toxic supervisor, and the other group had a calm, composed, and supporting supervisor. The toxic manager, as the name suggests, used harsh words to get simple updates or to convey straightforward instructions or deadlines, while the other supervisor was polite and used positive words and affirmations throughout the length of the task. At the end of the experiment, the toxic supervisor and his group were not able to complete the task assigned to them. Additionally, there were multiple mistakes, and the work done was of an inferior quality. On the other hand, the calm and composed motivator and his group had completed the task before time, and in the spare time, they also completed the documentation of the entire task.

Words can both ignite conflict and foster peace. Diplomatic language can help resolve disputes and build alliances, while inflammatory language can escalate tensions and provoke violence. Words can cause conflicts by misinforming, provoking, and polarising people. The power of language to shape perceptions and influence emotions means that words, when used irresponsibly or maliciously, can lead to significant, and sometimes violent, conflicts. Put simply, words can either start or end wars.

Recently, a lip reader explained what Cristiano Ronaldo says to himself repeatedly before a free kick or penalty: "You are the best. You know you're the best and you're going to score. It's going to be a goal; it's going to be a goal. You know it's going to be a goal." The result? He hits the goal almost every time. If the greatest footballer is taking the words spoken to himself so seriously, so should you.

Now that we've understood the power of words, what next? Well, here are a few things that are a must and should never be overlooked if you don't want to cause harm to yourself or others, and to use the power of words to your advantage.

Use Affirmative Language: Choose positive and empowering words. Instead of saying, "I can't do this," say, "I can learn to do this," or "I will give it my best."

Reframe Negative Thoughts: When you catch yourself in negative self-talk, reframe those thoughts. Turn "I'm failing" into "I'm learning and growing," or "This is an opportunity to improve."

Use Present Tense: Speak to yourself in the present tense as if the positive outcome is already happening. For example, say "I am becoming more confident every day" instead of "I will become more confident."

Be Kind and Compassionate: Treat yourself with the same kindness and compassion you would offer a friend. Avoid harsh criticism and self-judgement, and instead, use supportive and understanding language.

Set Positive Intentions: Begin your day with positive intentions. Tell yourself what you aim to achieve and how you want to feel. For example, "Today, I will stay focused and productive," or "I will handle challenges with grace."

Affirm Your Worth: Regularly affirm your self-worth and value. Statements like "I am worthy of success and happiness," or "I deserve to be treated with respect," can reinforce your self-esteem.

Encourage Yourself: Use motivational self-talk to boost your morale. Phrases like "I can handle this," "I am strong," or "I am capable of achieving my goals" can provide encouragement and drive.

Be Realistic and Honest: While positivity is important, it's also essential to be realistic. Acknowledge challenges and setbacks honestly, but pair them with constructive and positive language about how you will overcome them.

Practice Forgiveness: Use self-talk to forgive yourself for past mistakes. Saying "I forgive myself and am learning from my experiences" can help you move forward without lingering guilt or regret.

Celebrate Small Wins: Recognise and celebrate your small victories. Affirming these achievements, no matter how minor, can boost your confidence and keep you motivated.

Create a Mantra: Develop a personal mantra or set of positive affirmations that resonate with you. Repeat these regularly to reinforce a positive mindset.

Challenge Limiting Beliefs: Identify and challenge any limiting beliefs you hold about yourself. Use positive affirmations to counteract these beliefs and reinforce your potential.

By consistently using these practices, you can cultivate a positive and empowering inner dialogue that supports your mental well-being and personal growth.

ONE DAY OR DAY ONE

"Magic lies in the work you are avoiding."

- Khalil Gibran

"The day has just started. I have a lot of time."

"The curriculum has just begun, studies can wait."

"I have started writing a book, so what? It's Friday, time to pamper yourself with an ice cream and a night with Netflix."

"I have just paid for your gym membership. I can start in the coming week."

"I can't begin until I have all the details perfectly planned out. It has to be flawless from the start."

"I need to do more research to make sure I have the best approach before I start."

"I'll do it later. I'm just not in the mood right now,"

"I'll be more productive after a short break. I deserve to rest."

"I'll just check social media for a few minutes to clear my mind, then I'll get started."

"This task won't take long. I can easily finish it later tonight."

"It's too noisy right now. I'll start when it's quieter."

Do all the above statements or a few of them sound familiar? I'd be surprised if you say that you are not familiar with them. I mean it. Because, these statements are your free pass to do anything, which is nothing but a cheap shot of dopamine. This is nothing but procrastination. Your mind is giving you all these ready-to-use templates to be thrown against your motivation to walk out of a situation that demands focus, dedication, and sincerity.

Close your eyes, take a deep breath and ask yourself, at this moment, are you not completely aware of your goals, your priorities, the work you must complete, the book you must read, the workout that is long due? The task that is waiting on you, the long-pending wish that needs your attention and some thoughts to nurture it? You know, and you exactly know what you should be doing now, tomorrow morning, midday, evening, before bed, or at any given point of time. The biggest and most painful lie you have been telling yourself is, "I will do it tomorrow." You are old enough to know where you should be, what tasks or workouts or hobbies should consume your time and energy, and what after-effects it can attract if not done within time. The key is to make the move, to take the first step in any direction. It can be a small walk in the park or a hundred-mile ultra marathon; it all starts with one step. You think I am a robot? No, while I'm writing this chapter on a Friday night at 1:42 AM, I too have a Netflix account, Instagram, Facebook, Kindle, a few books waiting for me to move beyond the cover page, but I chose to write this chapter for you, my dear readers, who, if guided in the right direction, can do wonders in your lives. I tricked my brain to sit at my work desk before I could've crashed onto the couch with the TV remote next to me. I too have a 4K television with a plethora of subscriptions getting wasted, but I'm here. How? Let's first understand how your brain tricks you, then we will learn how to trick your brain.

How Your Brain Tricks You into Procrastination.

Our brains are incredibly adept at finding ways to procrastinate, often without us even realising it. The process is subtle, yet powerful, and it can derail our best intentions. Here are some common ways our brains trick us into procrastination:

1. **Rationalising Small Tasks:** Our brain often convinces us to prioritise minor tasks over more important ones. It whispers, "Just tidy up your workspace first; you'll be able to focus better." This seems logical, but it leads us down a path of small, inconsequential tasks that eat up our time and delay the main task.

2. **Seeking Perfection:** Perfectionism is another trick. Our brain tells us, "You can't start until you have everything perfectly planned out." This pursuit of perfection makes us delay starting because we feel unprepared. In reality, it's often better to start imperfectly and refine along the way (like how I started to write this book with one line under my notes).

3. **Underestimating Time:** A common procrasti-nation tactic is underestimating the time required for a task. Our brain reassures us, "This won't take long; you can easily finish it later." This leads to last-minute

rushes and increased stress, often resulting in lower-quality work.

4. **Distraction and Instant Gratification:** Our brains are wired to seek pleasure and avoid discomfort. This is why we might find ourselves saying, "I'll just check social media for a few minutes to clear my mind." What starts as a brief distraction can easily turn into a prolonged period of unproductive time.

5. **Overwhelm and Avoidance:** When faced with a large or daunting task, our brain can make us feel overwhelmed. It tells us, "There's so much to do; I don't even know where to start." This feeling of overwhelm makes us avoid the task altogether, preferring to tackle simpler, less intimidating activities. (Trust me, I had these feelings while starting many projects and tasks.)

6. **Justifying Delays:** Our brain is skilled at coming up with justifications for delays. It might say, "I'll be more productive after a short break," or, "I need to do more research before I can start." While breaks and preparation are important, they can become excuses for inaction if not managed properly.

7. **Fear of Failure:** Fear of failure is a powerful procrastination trigger. Our brain whispers, "What if you mess up? Better wait until you are sure you can do it perfectly." This fear prevents us from starting because we dread the possibility of not meeting our own or others' expectations.

8. **External Blame:** Sometimes, our brain shifts the blame to external factors to justify procrastination. It tells us, "I can't work on this now because I need

input from someone else," or, "It's too noisy right now." While external factors can be legitimate, they often serve as convenient excuses to delay tasks.

Recognising these tricks our brain plays on us is the first step towards overcoming procrastination. By being aware of these patterns, we can develop strategies to counteract them, such as breaking tasks into smaller steps, setting realistic deadlines, and creating a focused work environment. Overcoming procrastination requires conscious effort and self-awareness, but the rewards of increased productivity and reduced stress are well worth it.

I know it sounds highly relatable and super personal because we have all experienced it. As I said, you know what you should be doing at this very moment; it's just that you are not doing it because your brain is tricking you with all the above lame excuses, forcing you to choose the path of joy, instant gratification, and least resistance. Procrastination is a common challenge that affects many of us, often hindering our productivity and causing unnecessary stress. Despite our best intentions, the lure of distractions and the comfort of delaying tasks can be hard to resist. However, by understanding how our brains work and employing certain strategies, we can outsmart these tendencies and foster a more proactive mindset. It's time to be a little aware and reverse engineer the brain to choose what is right over what is comfortable.

Here Are Some Effective Ways to Trick Our Brains into Doing What Is Right

1. **Break Tasks into Smaller Steps:** One effective way to combat procrastination is to break large tasks into smaller, more manageable steps. Instead of thinking, "I need to write a report," trick your brain by focusing on smaller tasks like, "I'll write the introduction first." This makes the task feel less overwhelming and gives you a sense of accomplishment as you complete each step.

2. **Use the Five-Minute Rule:** The Five-minute rule suggests that if a task takes less than five minutes to complete, you should do it immediately. This not only helps you get small tasks out of the way quickly but also builds momentum for tackling larger tasks. Tell yourself, "I'll just spend five minutes on this," and you'll often find that once you've started, it's easier to keep going.

3. **Set Specific, Achievable Goals:** Setting specific, achievable goals helps focus your efforts and provides a clear roadmap. Instead of a vague goal like "work on project," set a specific goal like "write 500 words for the project by noon." Clear goals give your brain a concrete target to aim for, making it harder to justify procrastination.

4. **Create a Reward System:** Rewarding yourself for completing tasks can motivate your brain to stay focused. Promise yourself a small treat or break after finishing a task. For example, "Once I finish this chapter, I'll take a 15-minute break and do anything I like." This creates a positive association

with completing tasks and encourages you to stay on track. (But make sure the 15-minute break should not end up being a 2-hour, 15-minute break)

5. **Implement Time Blocking:** Time blocking involves scheduling specific blocks of time for different tasks throughout your day. By allocating time slots for particular activities, you create a structured routine that helps prevent procrastination. For instance, "From 9 to 10 AM, I'll work on my presentation." This helps your brain commit to focused work periods.

6. **Use Visualisation Techniques:** Visualise the benefits of completing your tasks and the consequences of not doing so. Picture yourself feeling accomplished and stress-free after finishing your work. Conversely, imagine the stress and guilt of procrastinating. This mental exercise can motivate your brain to take action now, rather than delay.

7. **Eliminate Distractions:** Identify and eliminate distractions in your work environment. This might mean turning off notifications, closing unnecessary browser tabs, or setting up a dedicated workspace. By reducing opportunities for distraction, you make it easier for your brain to focus on the task at hand.

8. **Practice Mindfulness and Self-Compassion:** Mindfulness helps you stay present and aware of your thoughts and feelings without judgement. When you notice procrastination tendencies, acknowledge them and gently steer yourself back to the task. Practicing self-compassion involves being kind to yourself when you slip up, which can reduce the negative emotions that fuel procrastination.

9. **Commit Publicly:** Sharing your goals with others can create a sense of accountability. Tell a friend, family member, or colleague about what you plan to accomplish, and ask them to check in on your progress. This external accountability can motivate your brain to follow through on commitments.

10. **Eat The Frog:** Tackle the most challenging task on your to-do list first thing in the morning when you are fresh with a well-rested mind and body and sufficient energy. This is known as "eating the frog." By getting the hardest task out of the way early, you set a productive tone for the day and reduce the likelihood of procrastination on other tasks.

To conclude, tricking your brain into doing what is right and avoiding procrastination involves a combination of strategies that address both the psychological and practical aspects of work. By breaking tasks into smaller steps, setting clear goals, creating a reward system, and eliminating distractions, you can train your brain to stay focused and productive. Implementing these techniques requires practice and patience, but over time, they can significantly reduce procrastination and improve your overall efficiency and well-being.

Procrastination is more than just a delay in action; it's a barrier that stands between us and our fullest potential. Each time we give in to the temptation of postponing our tasks, we surrender a piece of our dreams, goals, and self-worth. The cost of procrastination is not just lost time, but also missed opportunities and diminished self-confidence. However, this is not a battle you have to lose. Imagine the freedom and empowerment that come with breaking free from this cycle. Picture yourself living a life where you seize the day, where each moment is an opportunity to move closer to your aspirations.

The journey to overcoming procrastination is not about striving for perfection; it's about making consistent, deliberate progress. It's about recognising the power within you to change your habits and reclaim your time. Each small step you take towards tackling your tasks is a victory, a testament to your commitment to personal growth. Embrace the strategies you've learned—whether it's breaking tasks into smaller steps, setting clear goals, or creating a reward system—and believe in your ability to change.

Remember, the path to success is paved with small, consistent actions. A marathon begins with a single step. It's about taking that first bold step today, even when it feels challenging. Surround yourself with reminders of your goals, visualise your success, and celebrate your achievements, no matter how small. Procrastination may be a formidable opponent, but your determination and proactive mindset are far stronger.

Take charge of your life because your future self is counting on you. By conquering procrastination, you're not just improving your productivity; you're building a foundation for a more fulfilled, accomplished, and empowered you, and, moreover, everything, you respect yourself when you do what is right. The journey may be tough, but the rewards are immense. Step into your power, take control of your time, and watch as your life transforms in ways you never thought possible.

Take charge, my friend, you've got this!

THE TRUTH ABOUT SKILLS

"Build your skills, not your resume."

– Sheryl Sandberg

The world we are living in today, marked by relentless change and unpredictability, possessing a robust skill set is no longer a luxury but a necessity for survival. The job market, a landscape of ceaseless flux, demands more than mere qualifications; it requires adaptability, creativity, and a relentless pursuit of mastery. Today's economy doesn't just reward those who have knowledge, but those who know how to apply it dynamically across various contexts. It's not enough to simply be educated; one must be skilled in ways that are relevant and responsive to the rapid changes that define our times.

In this chapter, we delve into the essence of skills—not just as tools for employment, but as lifelines that empower us to navigate and thrive amidst the chaos. We will explore how developing a diverse array of skills can act as a shield against the volatility of the job market and as a sword to carve out new opportunities where none existed before. From technical proficiencies to soft skills, from critical thinking to emotional intelligence, the ability to learn and adapt has become the most valuable currency.

We uncover the transformative power of continuous learning and skill development, exploring how they forge resilience and unlock boundless opportunities in an uncertain world. In the face of automation and artificial intelligence, the unique capabilities that humans bring, such as creativity, empathy, and complex problem-solving, become our greatest assets. By investing in our skills, we not only enhance our employability but also build a foundation for lifelong growth and fulfilment.

Defining Skills in the Modern Context

In today's landscape, the definition of skills extends far beyond traditional notions. Skills encompass a wide range of abilities, competencies, and attributes that empower individuals to perform tasks effectively, solve problems creatively, and adapt to new challenges. Understanding what constitutes a skill in the modern context is essential for navigating the complexities of the job market and thriving in any professional environment.

What Are Skills?

Hard Skills: These are specific, teachable abilities that can be measured and defined. Examples include technical proficiencies like programming, data analysis, graphic design, and financial accounting. Hard skills are often acquired through formal education, training programmes, and hands-on experience. They are essential for performing specific tasks and are typically the focus of job descriptions and qualifications.

Soft Skills: Also known as interpersonal or people skills, soft skills are less tangible and harder to quantify. They include abilities such as communication, teamwork, problem-solving, and emotional intelligence. Soft skills are crucial for building relationships, fostering collaboration, and navigating the social dynamics of the workplace. They complement hard skills and often play a key role in determining an individual's overall effectiveness and success in their career.

The Evolution of Skills

Technological Advancements: The rapid pace of technological innovation has significantly altered the skill requirements in many industries. Automation, artificial intelligence, augmented reality, and digital transformation are reshaping job roles, making technical skills like coding, cybersecurity, and data science increasingly important.

Globalisation: As businesses operate on a global scale, cultural competence, foreign language proficiency, and the ability to work in diverse teams have become valuable assets. Understanding and navigating different cultural contexts is crucial for success in a globalised economy.

Changing Work Environments: The rise of remote work, gig economy, and freelance opportunities has shifted the focus towards skills that enable flexibility and self-management. Time management, digital communication, and the ability to work independently are more critical than ever.

Emphasis on Innovation and Creativity: In a world where information is readily accessible, the ability to think creatively and innovate is a significant differentiator. Skills in design thinking, creative problem-solving, and strategic planning are highly sought after in many fields.

By recognising the diverse and dynamic nature of skills in the modern context, you can better prepare yourself to meet the demands of today's job market. Embracing both hard and soft skills, staying attuned to industry trends, and continuously seeking opportunities for growth and development are essential strategies for building a resilient and adaptable skill set. In the following sections, we will explore how to cultivate these skills and leverage them to achieve professional and personal success.

The Role of Continuous Learning

Embracing a lifelong learning mindset is essential for staying relevant and competitive in the job market, as it allows individuals to adapt to new challenges, acquire emerging skills, and keep pace with industry innovations. Continuous learning fosters intellectual growth, enhances problem-solving abilities, and cultivates a sense of curiosity and resilience. By engaging in ongoing education—whether through formal training, online courses, or self-directed study—individuals can not only safeguard their careers against obsolescence, but also unlock new opportunities for personal and professional development, ensuring they remain agile and adaptable in an unpredictable world.

Practical Steps to Skill Development

Skill development is a strategic and continuous process that requires dedication, planning, and the right resources.

Here are practical steps to help you enhance your skill set effectively:

1. Self-Assessment

- **Identify Your Current Skills:** Start by listing the skills you already possess. This includes both hard and soft skills, as well as any specialised domain knowledge.

- **Determine Gaps and Needs:** Compare your current skills against those required in your desired field or role. Identify the gaps where you need improvement or learn entirely new skills.

2. Setting Goals

- **Short-Term Goals:** Set achievable, specific goals for the near future. These could include completing a course, obtaining a certification, or mastering a particular software or skill.

- **Long-Term Goals:** Define broader objectives that align with your career aspirations, such as transitioning to a new role, becoming an expert in your field, or acquiring a comprehensive set of skills.

3. Creating a Learning Plan

- **Outline Your Path:** Develop a clear, step-by-step plan to achieve your goals. This should include timelines, milestones, and the resources you will need.

- **Flexible Learning Paths:** Incorporate different learning methods, such as online courses, workshops, seminars, and practical experiences, to keep the process engaging and effective.

4. Leveraging Online Resources

- **E-Learning Platforms:** Utilise platforms like Coursera, Udemy, LinkedIn Learning, and Pluralsight to access a wide range of courses and tutorials.

- **Webinars and Podcasts:** Follow industry experts and thought leaders through webinars, podcasts, and online conferences to stay updated with the latest trends and insights.

5. Practical Application

- **Hands-On Practice:** Apply what you learn through projects, internships, volunteering, or freelancing. Real-world experience is invaluable in reinforcing new skills.

- **Experiment and innovate:** Don't be afraid to try new approaches and experiment with your skills in different contexts to deepen your understanding and adaptability.

6. Networking and Mentorship

- **Build a Network:** Connect with professionals in your field through networking events, social media, and professional organisations. Networking can provide valuable insights and opportunities.

- **Seek Mentorship:** Find mentors who can offer guidance, share their experiences, and provide feedback on your progress.

7. Feedback and Reflection

- **Regular Reviews:** Periodically review your progress against your goals. Adjust your learning plan as needed based on what you've learned and any changes in your career path or industry.

- **Reflect on Learning:** Take time to reflect on what you've learned and how you've applied it. This helps reinforce knowledge and identify areas for further improvement.

8. Staying Motivated

- **Celebrate Achievements:** Recognise and celebrate your milestones and accomplishments, no matter how small. This can boost your motivation and confidence.

- **Stay Curious:** Cultivate a mindset of curiosity and a love for learning. Always be on the lookout for new skills and knowledge that can enhance your personal and professional life.

By following these practical steps, you can systematically develop and refine your skills, positioning yourself for success in an ever-changing world. Continuous learning and skill development are not just about keeping up; they are about staying ahead and thriving in any environment.

As we navigate the ever-changing landscape of the modern world, the commitment to skill development stands as a beacon of hope and empowerment. Embracing a mindset of continuous learning not only equips us to face the uncertainties of the job market, but also enriches our lives with new possibilities and personal growth. Each skill we acquire, each challenge we overcome, adds to our resilience and adaptability, making us stronger and more capable.

The journey of lifelong learning is a testament to our ability to evolve and thrive amidst chaos. It is an affirmation of our potential to not just survive, but to excel and lead in our chosen fields. By investing in our skills, we open doors to new opportunities, forge meaningful connections, and build a foundation for sustained success and fulfilment.

Remember, the pursuit of knowledge and skills is a lifelong adventure—one that is as rewarding as it is challenging. Every step you take in expanding your capabilities brings you closer to your goals and dreams. Stay curious, stay dedicated, and, most importantly, stay inspired. In the end, it is our relentless pursuit of excellence that will light our path in an unpredictable world, transforming challenges into stepping stones and dreams into realities. Embrace the journey with an open heart and a determined spirit, for the world is yours to conquer.

DON'T MIND YOUR MIND!

Imagine waking up one morning to find an unruly roommate has taken over your house. This roommate seems to have no regard for your personal space or sanity. They move your belongings around without permission, creating disarray wherever they go. You find your keys in the fridge, your shoes in the bathtub, and important documents scattered across the floor. Their messes are not just physical; they leave emotional clutter too—doubts, anxieties, and worries strewn about like confetti.

You try everything to rein them in. You set strict rules, hoping to impose order. "No clutter in the living room!" you declare, only to find them hoarding newspapers and old magazines there the next day. You lock doors to keep them out of certain rooms, but they find ways to sneak in through windows you didn't even know were open. You plead with them to respect your space, but their chatter grows louder, drowning out your thoughts and disrupting your peace.

You resort to shouting in frustration, hoping to intimidate them into compliance. "Enough!" you yell, but they laugh it off, continuing to create chaos with a mischievous glint in their eye. The more you try to control them, the more defiant and chaotic they become. It's as if they thrive on your attempts to rein them in, finding amusement in your futile efforts.

Our minds are incredible, intricate systems capable of extraordinary creativity, problem-solving, and emotional depth. Yet, they can also be our biggest saboteurs, filling our heads with worries, doubts, and endless streams of thoughts that we can't seem to turn off. It's easy to believe that if we just try harder, we can control our thoughts and achieve a state of perfect mental clarity. But, much like the unruly roommate, attempting to control the mind often leads to more frustration and chaos.

Think about a time when you were trying to focus on an important task, but your mind kept drifting to unrelated worries and distractions. You might have told yourself to "focus" repeatedly, only to find your thoughts becoming even more scattered. This is a common experience for many of us. The harder we try to wrestle our thoughts into submission, the more they seem to slip through our fingers, like sand.

The mind has its own agenda, often driven by deep-seated habits and unconscious processes that we aren't even aware of. It's a whirlwind of thoughts, emotions, memories, and fantasies that can sweep us up and carry us away if we let it. The more we fight against this natural turbulence, the more exhausted and defeated we feel.

In this chapter, we'll explore the nature of the mind and why attempting to control it can be an exercise in futility. Instead of battling against our thoughts, we can learn to manage and deal with them effectively. By accepting the mind's inherent unpredictability, we can develop strategies to navigate our mental landscape with greater ease and resilience.

We'll delve into mindfulness, a practice that teaches us to observe our thoughts without getting entangled in them. We'll also discuss cognitive behavioural techniques that help us reframe negative thinking patterns, and Acceptance and Commitment Therapy (ACT), which encourages us to accept our thoughts and commit to actions that align with our values.

Consider the story of Emma, a successful professional who found herself paralysed by anxiety and self-doubt. She spent countless hours trying to suppress her negative thoughts, which only seemed to grow louder and more persistent. It wasn't until she began practicing mindfulness and accepting her thoughts without judgement that she found relief. By learning to coexist with her mind rather than control it, Emma was able to reclaim her peace and productivity.

Through real-life examples and practical exercises, this chapter will equip you with the tools to transform your relationship with your mind. You'll discover that it's not about silencing your thoughts, but about changing how you respond to them. By doing so, you can find greater balance, clarity, and fulfilment in your life.

The Nature of the Mind

Our minds are intricate universes within us, constantly buzzing with thoughts, emotions, and sensations. They are like vast landscapes where ideas bloom like flowers and memories dance like shadows. Yet, despite their richness and complexity, our minds can also be turbulent and unpredictable, akin to a stormy sea.

At the core of this complexity lies the dual nature of our thoughts. On one hand, our minds are capable of incredible creativity and problem-solving. They conceive of innovations, compose symphonies, and unravel the mysteries of the universe. Our minds are the architects of our dreams and the engines of our ambitions, propelling us forward with their boundless potential.

On the other hand, our minds can be our greatest adversaries. They often replay past traumas, amplify our fears, and magnify our insecurities. Like a restless child, the mind can wander into dark corners, conjuring scenarios that evoke anxiety or regret. It fixates on uncertainties and dwells on hypotheticals, spinning tales that may never come to pass. The mind's tendency to wander is not a flaw but a feature, a reflection of its innate curiosity and adaptability. It sifts through memories, making connections between seemingly unrelated events. It projects into the future, anticipating challenges and envisioning possibilities. This constant flux of thoughts is what makes our minds both exhilarating and exhausting to inhabit.

Attempting to control this ceaseless flow of thoughts is akin to trying to tame a wild river. It can be tempting to build dams and redirect its course, but ultimately, the river will find its way. Similarly, our minds resist confinement. They defy our attempts to impose order and structure. The more we struggle against their natural currents, the more tumultuous they become.

Accepting the nature of our minds does not mean resigning ourselves to chaos. Instead, it invites us to develop a different relationship with our thoughts. Rather than trying to control them, we can learn to observe them with curiosity and compassion. Through mindfulness practices and introspective reflection, we cultivate a deeper understanding of our mental landscapes.

Embracing the nature of our minds allows us to harness their potential while navigating their challenges with grace. By embarking on this journey of self-discovery and mental exploration, we can cultivate a greater sense of peace, clarity, and well-being in our lives.

The Illusion of Control

In the labyrinth of our minds, there exists a persistent illusion – that we have complete control over our thoughts and emotions. We cling to this belief, striving to manage every thought, suppress every doubt, and orchestrate every feeling. Yet, the more we grasp for control, the more elusive it becomes.

Our desire for control stems from a fundamental need for security and stability in an uncertain world. We seek to assert authority over our thoughts as a means of safeguarding our sense of self and protecting against discomfort. We impose rules and restrictions, hoping to steer our minds towards calm waters and clear skies.

Consider a moment when you tried to suppress a feeling of anger or anxiety, only to have it resurface with greater intensity later on. Or a time when you meticulously planned every detail of an important event, only to encounter unforeseen obstacles that derailed your efforts. These experiences highlight the limitations of our control over the unpredictable terrain of the mind.

The illusion of control not only creates inner turmoil but also perpetuates a cycle of stress and dissatisfaction. We become trapped in a perpetual struggle against our own thoughts, exhausting ourselves in pursuit of an unattainable ideal. Our quest for certainty blinds us to the inherent fluidity of life, preventing us from fully embracing its uncertainties and opportunities for growth.

What if, instead of striving for control, we chose to cultivate acceptance? Acceptance does not imply passivity or resignation, but rather a willingness to acknowledge and embrace the present-moment as it unfolds. It involves letting go of the need to manipulate outcomes and trusting in our capacity to navigate challenges with resilience and grace.

By releasing the illusion of control, we open ourselves to the transformative power of presence and compassion. We learn to surf the waves of our emotions, rather than resisting their swell. We discover that true strength lies not in mastering our minds, but in embracing their inherent complexity and beauty.

Techniques for Managing the Mind

Navigating the intricate landscape of our minds requires skillful techniques that honour the complexity of our inner experiences. Rather than seeking to control our thoughts and emotions, we can cultivate practices that promote awareness, resilience, and compassionate self-understanding. Here are some effective techniques for managing the mind:

Mindfulness Meditation: Mindfulness invites us to observe our thoughts and emotions with a gentle curiosity, without judgement or attachment. By practicing mindfulness meditation regularly, we develop greater awareness of our mental patterns and emotional triggers. This heightened awareness allows us to respond to challenges with clarity and composure, rather than reacting impulsively.

Breath Awareness: Our breath serves as a bridge between body and mind. By focusing on the sensations of our breath – its rise and fall, its rhythm, and depth – we can anchor ourselves in the present-moment. Breath awareness helps to calm the mind, reduce stress, and enhance our ability to regulate emotions.

Cognitive Restructuring: Cognitive restructuring involves identifying and challenging unhelpful thought patterns, such as negative self-talk or catastrophic thinking. By examining the evidence for and against these thoughts, we can develop more balanced and realistic perspectives. This technique empowers us to replace automatic, distorted thoughts with healthier alternatives that promote resilience and well-being.

Gratitude Practice: Cultivating a daily practice of gratitude shifts our focus from what is lacking in our lives to what we already have. By acknowledging and appreciating the positive aspects of our experiences, we foster a mindset of abundance and contentment. Gratitude practice has been shown to enhance mood, reduce stress, and improve overall psychological well-being.

Self-Compassion: Self-compassion involves treating ourselves with the same kindness and understanding that we would offer to a friend facing difficulty. It entails recognising our own humanity, embracing imperfections, and responding to ourselves with warmth and empathy during times of struggle. Self-compassion fosters resilience, reduces self-criticism, and promotes emotional healing.

Physical Exercise: Physical activity is not only beneficial for our physical health but also plays a crucial role in managing our mental well-being. Exercise releases endorphins, natural mood lifters, and reduces levels of stress hormones like cortisol. Engaging in regular exercise, whether through aerobic activities, yoga, or strength training, enhances mood, improves sleep, and boosts overall mental clarity.

Mindful Eating: Mindful eating involves paying attention to the sensory experience of eating, such as the taste, texture, and aroma of food, without distractions. By savouring each bite and tuning into our body's hunger and fullness cues, we can develop a healthier relationship with food and promote mindful decision-making around eating habits.

Setting Boundaries: Establishing clear boundaries in our personal and professional lives is essential for maintaining mental well-being. Boundaries help to protect our time, energy, and emotional resources from being depleted by external demands and obligations. By asserting our needs and limitations, we create space for self-care and cultivate healthier relationships with others.

Journaling: Writing down our thoughts, feelings, and experiences in a journal can be a powerful tool for self-reflection and emotional processing. Journaling allows us to gain clarity on our inner world, identify recurring patterns, and explore solutions to challenges. It serves as a safe space for expressing emotions, reducing rumination, and promoting psychological resilience.

Social Connection: Human beings are inherently social creatures, and meaningful connections with others play a crucial role in our mental and emotional well-being. Nurturing supportive relationships–whether with friends, family members, or community groups–provides opportunities for mutual empathy, validation, and emotional support. Social connection buffers against stress, enhances mood, and promotes a sense of belonging and resilience.

By integrating these techniques into our daily lives, we can cultivate a more balanced and compassionate relationship with our minds. Rather than striving for control, we embrace a journey of self-discovery and growth, fostering resilience, inner peace, and a deeper connection to ourselves and others.

Practical Exercises for Managing the Mind

Practicing mindfulness and developing cognitive resilience are essential components of effectively managing the complexities of our minds. Below are practical exercises designed to cultivate awareness, foster resilience, and promote emotional well-being. It may sound prescriptive, and I hate to write it in this form, but I want you to follow it as a prescription, word by word:

Mindful Breathing Exercise

- Find a quiet place where you can sit comfortably.

- Close your eyes and bring your attention to your breath.

- Notice the sensation of the breath as it enters and leaves your nostrils, or fills your lungs.

- Without trying to change your breath, simply observe its natural rhythm for a few minutes.

- If your mind wanders (which is natural), gently guide your focus back to the breath.

- Practice this exercise for 5-10 minutes daily to cultivate present-moment awareness and calm.

Thought Labelling Exercise

- Throughout your day, notice when you experience strong emotions or repetitive thoughts.

- Mentally label the emotion or thought without judgement. For example, "This is anxiety" or "I'm having a worry about the future."

- Acknowledge the thought or feeling without getting caught up in its storyline, or trying to change it.

- This practice helps create distance between yourself and your thoughts, reducing their impact on your emotions and behaviour.

Gratitude Journaling

- Set aside time each day to write down three things you are grateful for.

- Be specific and detailed in your entries, focusing on both big and small blessings in your life.

- Reflect on why you are grateful for each item and how it has positively impacted your day or your overall well-being.

- Regularly practicing gratitude enhances positive emotions, shifts your perspective towards abundance, and strengthens resilience against negative thoughts.

Self-Compassion Break

- Think of a situation in your life that is causing you stress or emotional discomfort.

- Place your hands over your heart, or adopt a gentle, comforting posture.

- Offer yourself words of kindness and understanding, such as, "May I be kind to myself in this moment," or "It's okay to struggle; I'm doing the best I can."

- Embrace your own imperfections and recognise that suffering is a part of the shared human experience.

- This exercise promotes self-compassion, reduces self-criticism, and cultivates a sense of inner warmth and acceptance.

Body Scan Meditation

- Lie down or sit comfortably in a quiet space.

- Close your eyes and bring your attention to different parts of your body, starting from your toes and moving upward to your head, or vice versa.

- Notice any sensations, tension, or discomfort in each area without trying to change them.

- Breathe deeply into each part of your body, allowing any tension to release with each exhale.

- This practice promotes relaxation, body awareness, and mindfulness of physical sensations.

Digital Detox

- Designate a specific period (e.g. one hour, one evening, or one day) to disconnect from digital devices and screens.

- Use this time to engage in activities that promote mindfulness and presence, such as reading a book, going for a walk in nature, or spending quality time with loved ones.

- Notice how reducing screen time impacts your mental clarity, mood, and ability to focus on the present-moment.

- Regular digital detoxes help reduce stress, improve sleep quality, and foster deeper connections with oneself and others.

These practical exercises are designed to be integrated into your daily routine, allowing you to cultivate mindfulness, nurture resilience, and foster a greater sense of well-being. By exploring these techniques with an open mind and a spirit of curiosity, you can empower yourself to effectively manage the complexities of your mind and enhance your overall quality of life.

To conclude, managing the mind is not about exerting control, but cultivating awareness, resilience, and compassion. Through mindfulness, cognitive strategies, and self-care practices, we can navigate life's complexities with greater ease and clarity.

By embracing techniques like mindfulness meditation, cognitive restructuring, and gratitude journaling, we enhance our ability to respond to challenges with wisdom and perspective. These practices empower us to nurture healthy relationships, regulate our emotions effectively, and promote overall well-being.

Remember, the journey of mind management is not about perfection, but progress. Each day presents opportunities to deepen our understanding of ourselves and strengthen our mental resilience. By integrating these techniques into our daily lives, we foster a harmonious relationship with our minds and embrace the beauty of our shared human experience.

Let's look at this journey with openness and curiosity, cultivating a mindset of growth and self-discovery. Together, we can harness the power of our minds to lead fulfilling and purposeful lives.

WHO'S YOUR COFFEE MATE?

Beforeyoujumptoconclusionsbasedonthetitle I chose for this chapter, the simple question here is, whom you share your coffee with. While coffee is symbolic, what I mean to ask is, when you have free time and you need to have a happy, stressful, or any kind of conversation, who is on your speed dial? In the midst of the chaos that defines our modern world, the environments we cultivate around us can serve as anchors of stability and clarity. Our surroundings—be it the physical spaces we inhabit or the social circles we move within—profoundly shape our thoughts, behaviours, and overall well-being. Just as a plant thrives in fertile soil with ample sunlight, so too do we flourish when our environments nurture our growth and align with our values. The energy, attitudes, and habits of those we interact with can uplift us or drag us down, making it crucial to consciously curate our surroundings. By choosing to surround ourselves with positivity, inspiration, and support, we set the stage for a life of resilience and fulfilment amidst the turbulence. Take a look at the below image carefully:

Even if it is printed in black and white, you can imagine how immensely important your surroundings are.

Surroundings

Surroundings are not only limited to the people you spend your time with; it also depends on the kind of discussions you engage in, the information you share with them, and the energy exchanged during these conversations. Additionally, consumption plays a significant role. What are you consuming while you are together? Is it coffee, tea, or alcohol? Or are you like me, where everyone around you, even your best friends, is consuming alcohol, and you are just regretting being there or hoping they will remain sane and sober after a few drinks? Frequently, occasionally, or rarely, we have all been in such situations because we are social animals and we need people around us to bounce off ideas, get motivated, sometimes just talk, or seek validation. While our intentions are noble, let's understand what the real impact is:

Let's begin with the biggest trend these days. Rather, most of us think that is the only way to socialise:

Social Drinking

In the tapestry of our surroundings, the culture of social drinking can weave threads of subtle, yet profound disruption. While often seen as a harmless way to unwind or connect with others, regular social drinking can slowly erode the foundation of a healthy environment. Initially, it might seem like an easy way to bond with colleagues, friends, or even strangers, but the repercussions often go unnoticed until they manifest in more serious forms. It can foster habits that cloud our judgement, dampen our productivity, and strain our relationships. The company we keep during these occasions significantly influences our behaviour, sometimes leading us down paths we wouldn't tread sober. This influence can be particularly insidious as it gradually shifts our norms and expectations about what constitutes healthy interaction and relaxation.

Moreover, social drinking can mask underlying issues, allowing us to temporarily escape rather than address the challenges we face. Over time, the conviviality of shared drinks can give way to dependencies and conflicts, creating a ripple effect that impacts our mental and physical well-being. The regular presence of alcohol in social settings can make it difficult to establish meaningful connections without its crutch and can lead to a cycle where socialising becomes synonymous with drinking. To truly thrive in a chaotic world, it's essential to recognise the influence of social drinking on our lives and strive to surround ourselves with activities and people that promote clarity, purpose, and positive growth. By consciously choosing environments and companions that uplift and inspire us, we can cultivate a lifestyle that supports our highest potential, free from the subtle yet pervasive pull of social drinking.

I'm writing this chapter at a coffee shop, and there is a bar next to this coffee shop and a park too. Where I call my friends to meet up, at what time, and what we will consume will define the quality of our conversation. Shocking, an eye-opener, or a farce? While you process the text above, let's look at some additional aspects we should consider about our surroundings:

Social Influence

Social influence profoundly shapes our behaviours, attitudes, and decisions, often without us even realising it. The people we surround ourselves with establish norms and expectations that we unconsciously adopt, setting the standards for what we consider acceptable or desirable. Positive relationships provide emotional support, accountability, and motivation, encouraging us to pursue our goals and maintain healthy habits. Conversely, negative influences can lead to detrimental behaviours and increased stress. By carefully curating our social circles, we can harness the power of social influence to foster personal growth, emotional well-being, and overall success in navigating the complexities of life.

Impact on Productivity

The impact of our surroundings on productivity is profound and multifaceted. A well-organised, aesthetically pleasing environment can enhance focus and efficiency, reducing distractions and promoting a clear mind. Natural light, comfortable seating, and minimal clutter contribute to a workspace that supports sustained attention and creative thinking. Conversely, a chaotic or cluttered environment can impede concentration, increase stress, and lead to procrastination. Moreover, the presence of inspiring elements, such as art or plants, can stimulate motivation and positivity, further boosting productivity. By thoughtfully designing our surroundings, we can create an atmosphere that not only facilitates work but also nurtures our overall well-being, leading to more consistent and high-quality output.

Motivation and Inspiration

Spending time with the wrong people can have a profound negative impact on motivation and inspiration. Negative attitudes, lack of ambition, and pessimism among companions can erode our own enthusiasm and belief in our goals. When surrounded by individuals who prioritise leisure over personal growth, or who engage in behaviours that contradict our aspirations, we may find ourselves distracted from our ambitions and less driven to pursue them. Moreover, a lack of support or encouragement from these relationships can lead to self-doubt and a diminished sense of confidence in our abilities. Toxic relationships or environments can drain our energy and mental resources, leaving us feeling depleted and demotivated. Overall, the company we keep significantly influences our mindset and motivation, highlighting the importance of surrounding ourselves with supportive, positive influences who inspire us to strive for our highest potential. Just for your information, while I'm writing this book, I do not have even a single person who would discourage me in my goal; rather, I unfriended such people before I became a writer. Food for thought.

Personal Growth

Spending time with the wrong people can stagnate or hinder our personal growth in profound ways. Negative influences can instil limiting beliefs, discourage risk-taking, and hinder our willingness to explore new opportunities or challenges. In environments where complacency or mediocrity prevail, there may be little encouragement for self-improvement or pursuing ambitious goals. Toxic relationships can drain emotional energy, leading to feelings of frustration or self-doubt that impede progress. Moreover, lacking positive role models or mentors can deprive us of valuable guidance and inspiration needed for personal development. Conversely, surrounding ourselves with supportive, motivated individuals who share our values and aspirations can foster an environment conducive to growth, providing encouragement, constructive feedback, and opportunities for learning and advancement. Thus, the company we keep plays a crucial role in shaping our personal growth trajectory, influencing our mindset, goals, and overall potential for success.

Energy and Vibes

Spending time with the wrong people can deeply impact our energy and vibes. Negative individuals, or those who consistently emit pessimism, cynicism, or judgement, can create an atmosphere of negativity that permeates our own energy. Their constant complaints, criticism, or lack of enthusiasm can drain our positivity and leave us feeling emotionally exhausted. Toxic relationships, characterised by drama or conflict, can also contribute to a sense of unease and instability, disrupting our emotional equilibrium and sapping our energy reserves. Conversely, being around positive, supportive individuals who radiate optimism and encouragement can uplift our spirits and recharge our energy levels. Choosing to surround ourselves with people who foster a positive atmosphere can significantly enhance our overall well-being and contribute to a more harmonious and fulfilling life.

Sense of Belonging

Spending time with the wrong people can deeply affect our sense of belonging. When surrounded by individuals whose values, interests, or behaviours do not align with our own, we may feel misunderstood or disconnected. Negative interactions or exclusion from social activities can evoke feelings of loneliness and isolation. Moreover, if the company we keep does not provide emotional support or validation, we may struggle to feel accepted or valued within that group. Over time, this can lead to a diminished sense of belonging and a longing for genuine connections with people who share our beliefs and aspirations. Therefore, choosing to invest time and energy in relationships that foster mutual respect, understanding, and shared experiences is essential for nurturing a strong sense of belonging and fulfilment in our social circles.

That is a lot of information and perspective, isn't it? While all the above observations are personal and social, we really need to be protective about our surroundings and our companions. Get one thing straight, and there is no easy way of expressing it: you don't get to choose your family, but you can control whom and where you are spending your quality time with, the time of your life that you can never earn back. The time that is precious, rather invaluable. Who is that friend or colleague or your relative you are just tolerating rather than enjoying or learning something from? Figure out the people, after meeting whom, you feel low, negative, or lethargic. Who's that one friend who throws tantrums at you when you wish to meet and behaves like extending a favour by meeting you, and yet, you hardly get some direction post meeting? Time to pull the plug; such people, surroundings, and environments do not serve any purpose. Rather express some self-love, pick up that long-pending hobby, or read a book.

Bless you!

SECURE THE MINIMUM

*"If I cannot do great things,
I can do small things in a great way."*

\- Martin Luther King, Jr.

We all know time is ticking. Seconds turn to minutes, minutes to hours, hours into days, and days into life. You are God's most powerful creature, endowed with limitless potential. Each moment that passes is an opportunity, a chance to shape your destiny and leave your mark on the world. Yet, in the whirlwind of our chaotic lives, it's easy to lose sight of our capabilities and the significance of our actions. The regret of a life lived beneath our potential, of having had the time and opportunity but not making the most of it, is a heavy burden.

Time is the most precious resource we have; once it passes, it can never be reclaimed. Every action we take within that time moulds our future and defines our legacy. This chapter is about recognising the profound value of time and the importance of securing the minimum each day. By establishing small, powerful habits that anchor us, we can transform fleeting moments into meaningful progress. These daily actions ensure that, despite the chaos around us, we live each day with purpose, making every second count and stepping closer to realising our true potential.

The pain of discipline is far less than the pain of regret. We all have days when the sun doesn't shine as brightly, when motivation wanes, and challenges seem insurmountable. Yet, it's precisely on these days that our actions matter most. By identifying a few key things you must do each day, you create a blueprint for success. These small, consistent actions, no matter how simple, are your daily commitment to your future self. They are the anchors that keep you steady amidst life's turbulence. When you can look back on your day and see that you have taken these essential steps, you can call it a day well lived. It's not about perfection or grand achievements; it's about steady progress and knowing that, every day, you are moving closer to the life you envision.

For your information, the "Secure the Minimum" term is solely coined by me based on practice and experience. Let's understand what "Secure the Minimum" is all about. This concept revolves around identifying and committing to a set of fundamental tasks that ensure you are consistently progressing toward your goals. These tasks are your non-negotiables, the minimum you must achieve each day to consider it a success. The beauty of this approach is its flexibility—your "Secure the Minimum" list is uniquely yours and can be tailored to your specific ambitions. For instance, the daily essentials for a future athlete might include a rigorous workout, balanced nutrition, and adequate rest. In contrast, a budding writer's list might focus on dedicated writing time, reading for inspiration, and networking with fellow writers. Below are a few examples to help you craft your own "Secure the Minimum" list, but remember, it's all about what aligns best with your personal goals and aspirations.

Just for contextual understanding, here is how my secure the minimum list looks like:

Morning Meditation: Starting the day with 10 minutes of mindfulness to centre myself. If time allows, it goes up to 15 minutes, and even 30 minutes on weekends.

Exercise: Engaging in at least 30 minutes of physical activity to keep my body healthy. It includes a brisk walk or slow-paced jog. If I can't make it to the gym any day, then body-weight exercises and power stretching.

Healthy Eating: Ensuring I consume balanced and nutritious meals throughout the day, basically protein and fibre-rich meals, and not eating after sunset.

Gratitude Practice: Taking a moment to reflect on a million things I'm grateful for and listing them down as a part of my daily journal.

Journaling: Summary of how the day was, celebrating achievements for the day, and planning for the day ahead. Also, writing down positive affirmations. How transformative journaling can be, please read more on this in the Timeless Wisdom chapter.

Learning: Dedicating ten minutes to reading or learning something new.

A word a day: Learning a new word every day. It takes a minute, but it improves my vocabulary.

Sunlight: Stand under the sun for 10 minutes a day.

Reading: Reading fifteen pages a day, one book a week and post the review on Instagram on @ mimimumauthorspeaks

Spiritual Learning: Reading at least one verse from the "Bhagwat Geeta" for spiritual connect and wisdom.

Writing: I don't write every day. However, this is either about writing or about research for my future publications.

Connection: Reaching out to a loved one or a friend to maintain meaningful relationships.

Note: This list does not include all the tasks on auto-pilot, such as office work, bathing, brushing my teeth, household chores, etc.

By securing the minimum each day, you create a foundation of success that builds momentum over time. These small, consistent actions serve as a compass, guiding you through the chaos and ensuring you stay aligned with your true potential. Remember, it's not about grand gestures or perfection; it's about steady, intentional progress. As you refine and commit to your own "Secure the Minimum" list, you'll find that each day, no matter how turbulent, can be a step forward. Embrace this practice, and you'll cultivate a life of purpose, resilience, and fulfilment.

TIMELESS WISDOM

In the midst of chaos, there is also opportunity.

- Sun Tzu

As we come to an end of this journey, this final chapter is not just a conclusion, but a gateway to integrating timeless truths into our everyday existence. Here, we distil the essence of what it means to live mindfully, to cherish simplicity, and to cultivate a sense of purpose amidst the noise. These are not grandiose philosophies, but practical insights—collected from the tapestry of human experience—that will guide you through the turbulence, helping you to reclaim tranquillity and clarity in every moment. Let these pearls of wisdom be your compass as you navigate the intricate dance of today's world, grounding you in the present and illuminating the path forward.

Stop being a prisoner of your past and become the master sculptor of your future. I've endured countless betrayals and accusations, faced deception, and been exploited because of my trusting nature. I could dwell on these experiences, allowing them to bury me in the shadows of my past. Or, I can rise above, setting my sights higher and giving those who wronged me countless reasons to envy my success. The choice is mine. Likewise, you cannot move forward while constantly looking back.

Doing so will only lead to stumbling, or worse. There's a reason why the windshield is larger than the rearview mirror—focus on the expansive horizon ahead, not the narrow glimpse of what's behind.

Overthinking is a thief of joy, robbing us of peace and clarity. In our minds, we magnify problems, crafting elaborate scenarios of what could go wrong. This mental maze traps us in a cycle of worry and fear, making us suffer far more in our imagination than reality ever could. The truth is most of our anxieties never come to pass. The actual events are rarely as daunting as the monsters we conjure up in our heads. Life, in its essence, is often simpler and kinder than the stories we tell ourselves. By recognising this, we can free ourselves from the grip of overthinking and find solace in the present-moment, where challenges are tangible, and solutions are within reach.

Tackling hard things first is a powerful strategy that can transform your daily life. When we face the tasks that seem insurmountable, the ones that loom large in our minds, we reclaim our sense of control and accomplishment. "Eat that Frog," as they describe it. Imagine waking up each day with a daunting challenge ahead of you—a task so big that it casts a shadow over everything else. Postponing it doesn't diminish its presence; it grows larger, more intimidating, gnawing at the edges of your peace and productivity. By confronting these difficult tasks head-on, you dismantle their power over you. The moment you dive into them, you begin to chip away at their enormity, discovering that they are not as insurmountable as they appeared. Each step forward, no matter how small, is a victory, and with each victory, your confidence builds. Once you've conquered these big tasks, you liberate yourself. The rest of the day feels lighter, the smaller tasks seem effortless, and you can truly immerse yourself in your activities without the nagging dread of unfinished business. This proactive approach not only boosts your efficiency but also enhances your overall well-being, freeing your mind to fully enjoy the present-moment. So, dare to do the hard things first. Embrace the challenge, rise to the occasion, and let the sense of accomplishment set you free for the rest of the day.

Setting measurable goals is crucial for turning dreams into reality. Saying, "I wish to write a book one day" is an admirable aspiration but lacks the concrete steps needed to achieve it. In contrast, "I will write 2,500 words a day" transforms that wish into a clear, actionable plan. Measurable goals provide a roadmap, breaking down a monumental task into manageable workpieces. Each day, as you hit your word count, you build momentum and confidence, seeing tangible progress. This accountability pushes you to show up and transforms abstract desires into achievable plans. By setting and committing to these goals, you turn distant dreams into daily achievements, making your ultimate aspiration entirely attainable.

The "App" culture, with its obsession over using apps for everything from tracking water intake to counting calories and monitoring sleep, can often feel like a waste of time. While these apps promise precision and convenience, they can also add unnecessary complexity and distraction to our lives. There's something inherently grounding and straightforward about using classic pen and paper. Writing down your goals, tracking your habits, and noting your progress with a simple journal can foster a deeper connection to your daily routines. It encourages mindfulness and presence, allowing you to engage more fully with your actions, rather than getting lost in a sea of digital data. Embrace the simplicity of pen and paper, and reclaim the art of mindful living.

Don't wait for the perfect time; the best time to start anything was yesterday, the second best time is now. This very moment is the ideal time to hit the gym, pursue a long-term hobby, launch your business, or begin writing a book. Perfection is an illusion, and waiting for the perfect day—one where you've slept eight hours, woke up effortlessly at 5 AM, laced up your jogging shoes, and ran a marathon—will never happen; it will only keep you stagnant. That flawless day will never come. Stop wasting time on excuses and distractions, and dive into the real work. Embrace the imperfect now, and let your actions today pave the way for your future success.

The quickest path to achieving your goals is often found by moving slowly. In our fast-paced world, it's tempting to rush toward our objectives, believing that speed equates to success. However, true accomplishment requires a steady and deliberate pace. For instance, people are writing books using Chat GPT and other online writing tools, and here I am taking five months to research, eleven months to write, four months to edit the book you are reading now. When you genuinely commit to a goal, approach it with a slow but unwavering stride. This method allows you to maintain your energy and enthusiasm, preventing the exhaustion and burnout that can derail even the most passionate pursuits. By pacing yourself, you not only ensure a sustainable journey but also foster deeper learning and growth along the way. Embrace the power of patience, and you'll find that each step, no matter how measured, brings you closer to your dreams with clarity and resilience.

If you can conceive it, you can achieve it. Every great accomplishment begins as a mere thought in someone's mind. When you allow your imagination to envision a goal, you set the stage for its realisation. Belief in your ideas fuels your determination and action, transforming abstract concepts into tangible outcomes. With unwavering focus and relentless effort, what once seemed like a distant dream becomes an attainable reality. Trust in the power of your thoughts, for they are the seeds from which success grows. Just to let you know, this book started with a single line, "how to live in this chaotic world," in my notes.

People are comfortable with you when you fit into the mould of normalcy. Those who live in mediocrity often expect you to remain at their level. When you share ideas that aim to elevate you from mediocrity to greatness, they will bombard you with excuses, doubts, and discouragements. This negativity can erode your ambition if you allow it. Choosing the path of greatness often means you must be prepared to lose some people in your life. The harsh reality is that many do not appreciate seeing others surpass them in achieving something extraordinary. Pursuing greatness requires resilience, a strong sense of self, and the willingness to let go of relationships that hinder your progress. Surround yourself with those who inspire and support your dreams, and remember that the journey to greatness is often a solitary, but deeply rewarding one.

Avoid multitasking at all costs, whether you're dealing with tasks you love or those you despise. From personal experience, I've learned the hard way that multitasking is counterproductive. When I first began writing, I often sipped coffee as I worked, thinking it enhanced my process. Over time, I realised that I was neither fully enjoying my writing nor savouring my coffee. Now, as I write this, I made sure to finish my coffee beforehand so I can dedicate my full attention to crafting this message for you. If you have multiple tasks to complete, start by identifying the most challenging one that requires the most energy and tackle it first. Consider the interdependence of your tasks and plan accordingly, but always avoid doing two things simultaneously. Task-switching consumes more energy and time than focusing on one task at a time. By dedicating your full attention to each task, you enhance both the quality of your work and your overall productivity.

Change is the only constant in life. In a world that is perpetually evolving, change remains the one steadfast certainty. Embracing change allows us to adapt, grow, and thrive amidst uncertainty. It challenges us to leave our comfort zones, fostering resilience and innovation. Understanding that change is inevitable empowers us to face it with a positive outlook, transforming potential obstacles into opportunities for growth. By accepting and navigating change, we can continuously improve ourselves and our circumstances, keeping pace with the ever-shifting landscape of life.

You are never too old to achieve anything—age is just a number. Society often imposes limits based on age, but true potential knows no such boundaries. Whether you're pursuing a new career, learning a new skill, or embarking on a personal adventure, your age does not define your capability. Every stage of life brings unique experiences and wisdom that can be leveraged to reach new heights.

Embrace the mindset that it's never too late to follow your dreams, set new goals, and make meaningful contributions. Your journey is yours alone, and as long as you have the passion and determination, age becomes an irrelevant factor in the pursuit of your aspirations.

Actions define priorities - if you want to see your future, look at what you are doing now. The choices you make each day reflect what you truly value and shape the trajectory of your life. For instance, if you spend hours scrolling through social media, it indicates a priority on passive consumption rather than active creation. On the other hand, if you dedicate time to working on your goals, whether it's learning a new skill, exercising, or advancing your career, you are setting the foundation for future success. Your daily actions are the clearest indicators of where you are headed. By consciously choosing activities that align with your aspirations, you pave the way for a future that reflects your true desires and ambitions.

No Holidays to Success - Success doesn't recognise weekends. If you truly aspire to achieve greatness, you have to work consistently, embracing every day as an opportunity to move closer to your goals. Think of this relentless pursuit not as a source of stress but as a journey of growth. The initial discomfort and pressure only feel overwhelming until you adapt and find your rhythm. If the burden feels too heavy, it's okay to scale back your efforts momentarily—just don't stop. Keep moving forward, even if it's at a slower pace. Success is a marathon, not a sprint, and your unwavering dedication, day in and day out, will eventually lead you to triumph.

Consistency is the only key. Consistency is the bamboo plant of personal growth—patiently nurturing your dreams with steady effort. For the first five years, the bamboo spends its time developing a deep and intricate root system beneath the soil before breaking through the surface. During this period, it might seem like nothing is happening, but the farmer knows that true growth is occurring out of sight. The farmer's patience and unwavering care, watering and tending to the bamboo every single day, are akin to your consistent actions laying the foundation for future success. When the bamboo finally emerges, it can grow up to 90 feet in just a few weeks, symbolising the exponential progress that follows consistent effort. Does that mean the bamboo took a few weeks to grow? No, it means the bamboo took five years and a few weeks to reach this point. Remember, greatness is often cultivated in the unseen moments of persistence, just like the resilient bamboo that stands tall and unwavering, reaching for the sky. Believe in the beauty of your dreams and keep taking actions, no matter how small or insignificant; they will all show up in the big picture one day.

How Much is Enough? The Evil Called Abundance. In the relentless pursuit of wealth, we often lose sight of what truly matters. The allure of money, real estate, luxury, and material possessions can become a never-ending cycle of accumulation. No matter how much you acquire, it never seems to be enough. This endless chase can consume your life, leaving you perpetually unsatisfied. Take a moment to pause and reflect. Remember, no amount of money can buy back your health or your youth. The real treasures in life are not material but intangible—good health, meaningful relationships, and inner peace. These are the things that truly enrich our lives and give us lasting fulfilment. By constantly striving for more, you risk sacrificing the present for an elusive future. Embrace contentment and recognise the value of what you already have. Balance your ambitions with gratitude and mindfulness, ensuring that your pursuit of abundance doesn't overshadow the irreplaceable aspects of your life.

The General Prescription: stop learning from the reels and be real. "In a world bombarded with fleeting, superficial advice from endless social media reels or short videos, it's crucial to anchor yourself in reality. Instead of getting lost in the noise, focus on authentic experiences and genuine human connections. Engage deeply with your surroundings, nurture face-to-face relationships, and immerse yourself in activities that bring true joy and fulfilment. Life's most valuable lessons come from real-life challenges, meaningful interactions, and personal growth, not from quick-fix tips and curated online personas. Embrace the chaos with a grounded perspective, and let your own experiences be your greatest teacher."

Fair amount of care: Self-Love | Amidst the chaos of life, self-love and self-care are paramount. Just as an air hostess instructs you to put on your own mask before assisting others, prioritise your well-being to effectively support those around you. Avoid the trap of burnout from overwhelming expectations and responsibilities. Make time for yourself, indulge in activities that recharge your spirit, and set healthy boundaries. By nurturing yourself first, you build the strength and resilience needed to navigate life's challenges and truly be there for others.

The power of routine: The power of routine lies in its ability to bring order to chaos. Establishing a daily routine creates a sense of stability and predictability, allowing you to manage life's uncertainties with greater ease.

By consistently engaging in regular activities, you build habits that enhance productivity, reduce stress, and improve overall well-being. Routines provide a framework that frees your mind from constant decision-making, enabling you to focus on what truly matters. Embrace the power of routine to create a balanced, purposeful life amidst the chaos.

Self-Improvement Plan: The Real SIP. In a world that favours quick fixes, genuine self-improvement involves hard work and dedication rather than chasing trends. It requires honest self-reflection, setting meaningful goals, and developing resilience. A solid self-improvement plan focuses on creating specific, measurable, achievable, relevant, and time-bound (SMART) goals. It includes evaluating your strengths and weaknesses, breaking goals into actionable steps, seeking support, and regularly reviewing progress. Emphasising a growth mindset and integrating self-care ensures sustainable, long-term development and overall well-being. It's time to invest in the real SIP.

No search engine for life: There is no search engine for life. Relying on online searches, especially for health-related concerns, often leads to unnecessary stress and anxiety. Instead of turning to 'social media university' certified doctors for validation, seek advice from real experts. Want to lose weight? Consult a nutritionist. Need help with financial planning? Talk to a financial adviser. Experiencing troubling symptoms? Visit a healthcare professional. Your health is your most valuable asset, and no amount of money can buy it back. Prioritise your well-being by trusting qualified experts who can provide accurate, personalised guidance and care.

2 Day Rule: "The 2-Day Rule is a simple yet powerful tool to maintain consistency in your habits and routines. It states that you should never allow yourself to skip a positive habit for more than two consecutive days. Whether it's exercising, meditating, or working on a personal project, the 2-Day Rule helps you stay on track without feeling overwhelmed. Missing one day is understandable; life happens. But allowing a second day to pass can quickly lead to a downward spiral. By adhering to this rule, you cultivate discipline and resilience, ensuring that minor setbacks don't derail your long-term goals."

5-minute rule: The 5-Minute Rule is a practical strategy to overcome procrastination and build momentum. When faced with a task that feels overwhelming or unappealing, commit to working on it for just five minutes. This brief time commitment makes starting much easier and often leads to continuing beyond the initial five minutes. The rule leverages the psychology of motivation, turning daunting tasks into manageable ones and helping you break through inertia. By consistently applying the 5-Minute Rule, you can tackle even the most challenging tasks with less resistance and greater productivity.

Many people start, but you must finish what you started. Many people start, but true success comes from finishing what you start. Starting is easy; it's the initial burst of enthusiasm and excitement. However, seeing things through to completion requires perseverance, discipline, and a strong commitment to your goals. Challenges and distractions will inevitably arise, but pushing through them is what sets achievers apart. By consistently finishing what you begin, you build resilience, confidence, and a track record of accomplishment. Remember, the value lies not just in the beginning but in the completion of your endeavours.

Journaling: Scribble Your Way to Self-Discovery: Journaling is a powerful and transformative practice that allows you to capture your thoughts, emotions, and experiences in a tangible form. By putting pen to paper, you create a space for self-reflection, helping to clarify your goals, track your progress, and understand your inner world. This daily habit encourages mindfulness as it requires you to pause and consider your feelings and actions. Over time, journaling can reveal patterns in your behaviour, illuminate your strengths and areas for growth, and foster a deeper connection with yourself. It's a personal sanctuary where you can express your dreams, confront your fears, and celebrate your achievements. Through the act of journaling, you transform abstract thoughts into concrete insights, empowering you to live more intentionally and purposefully.

Celebrate small wins. Celebrating small wins is essential for maintaining motivation and fostering a positive mindset. Acknowledging milestones, such as one week, one month, or three months of giving up smoking or drinking, reinforces your progress and boosts your confidence. Each celebration releases dopamine, the 'feel-good' neurotransmitter, creating a sense of reward and accomplishment. This positive reinforcement makes it easier to continue your journey and overcome challenges. By celebrating small wins, you create a cycle of positivity and momentum, encouraging you to stay committed to your goals and paving the way for long-term success.

Clean up: Keeping your desk, workspace, and home. Being clean isn't just about physical tidiness; it's about mental clarity. According to Japanese philosophy, a clean environment reflects and promotes a clear mind. When your surroundings are organised, you experience less stress and distraction, allowing you to focus better on your tasks. This practice instils a sense of discipline and order, enhancing productivity and overall well-being. By regularly cleaning and decluttering, you create a serene space that fosters creativity, reduces anxiety, and promotes a harmonious balance between your inner and outer worlds.

Magical mornings. If you too, like the younger me, are ignoring the magic and the power of mornings, please don't. The power and the energy that the morning and the fresh air give you are unmatched and unbeatable, and I have been absolutely stupid to ignore this almost halfway through my life. If you can embrace the mornings and make the most out of it, and if your work schedule allows you to do so, please do yourself a favour and start getting up early. By saying that, I don't want you to join any 5, 6, 7 AM Club. All I want you to do is to take charge of your mornings and make the most out of it. Just give it a thought right now. If you are getting up at 9 or 10 AM, this getting up late is literally carried over throughout your day. If you're getting up late, you are starting your day late, you are eating late, and you are sleeping late. Now, if you switch your 8 AM routine to a 5 AM routine, you have three extra hours, and you're getting up early, getting more oxygen, and sleeping early. I think these arguments are enough for you to at least try and get up early. I don't expect someone who wakes up at eight, nine, or ten in the morning to suddenly start rising at five. However, there's a gradual approach that can help you achieve this. To shift your wake-up time sustainably, begin by waking up just five minutes earlier each day. For example, if you usually wake up at 9 AM, try getting up at 8:55 AM on the first day, then 8:50 AM the next day, and so on. By consistently adjusting your wake-up time in small increments, you'll eventually reach your goal of waking up at 7 AM in about 12 days. As they say, start your morning right, and you'll set the stage for a successful day.

The Transformative Power of Prayers: Prayer serves as a powerful tool for finding solace and clarity amidst the chaos of life. It transcends religious boundaries, offering a universal way to express gratitude, seek guidance, and find inner peace. The importance of prayer lies in its ability to centre our thoughts, calm our minds, and connect us to something greater than ourselves. By setting aside moments for prayer, we create a sacred space for reflection and renewal. This practice can be deeply satisfying, providing a sense of purpose and grounding, while fostering resilience and hope in times of adversity. Moreover, prayer encourages mindfulness and introspection, helping us to navigate challenges with grace and strength. Whether through structured rituals or spontaneous conversations with the divine, the act of praying can be a powerful anchor, offering comfort and a profound sense of connection in our increasingly hectic lives.

Trust in "His" plans. Believe that God has a plan for everyone, including you. Just as He ensures that even a bird sleeping on a tree does not fall, trust that He will not abandon you in your struggles. This divine assurance means you are never truly alone, no matter how chaotic life may seem. Embrace faith and let it guide you through the uncertainties, knowing that there is a higher purpose at play. Trust in God's plan and find peace in the journey, secure in the knowledge that you are cared for and protected.

"This too shall pass." In challenging times, when the going gets tough, remember that difficulties are temporary. An alternate perspective is that when the going gets difficult, the difficult get going. Life's trials are inevitable; not every day will be a Sunday, and you won't always be in perfect health—mentally or physically—to start anything new. Yet, these moments of hardship are fleeting. Embrace the struggle, knowing it will eventually fade. Hold on to the resilience within you and remind yourself that, no matter how tough it gets, this too shall pass.

"In closing, remember that living amidst chaos is not about avoiding challenges, but about harnessing the power within to navigate them with grace. As you journey forward, may these insights serve as a compass, guiding you towards clarity, resilience, and profound self-discovery. Embrace each day as an opportunity to grow, to thrive, and to find meaning in every moment. This chapter is not just a guide; it's a catalyst for transforming chaos into wisdom, and for living a life that is authentically yours."

This is not the end. Your new, enriching, fulfilling, and meaningful life has just begun…

If this book has helped you in any manner, I'd love to hear about it at @minimalauthorspeaks on Instagram.

I've tried summarising our entire journey through this poem. My first poem ever, dedicated to all you beautiful souls out there!

A Journey Through the Chaos

In the quiet of the night, when doubts invade,

Remember, life's a journey we've all made.

From chaos to calm, through valleys deep,

We find our strength in promises we keep.

We question, "Why me?" in times of strife,

Yet, every challenge shapes our life.

In a world where masks and screens prevail,

Seek truth within, let your spirit sail.

Addiction's grasp, comfort's deceit,

We've battled foes, both fierce and sweet.

But there's a fire within our core,

A light that guides us to much more.

Through financial woes and minimal gains,

We learn to dance in life's refrains.

In diet, dead, and muscles strained,

In every loss, something's gained.

Habits form the paths we tread,
Meditation soothes the restless head.
Discipline leads us to our throne,
Gratitude makes us feel at home.

Words, so powerful, carve our way,
Decide today, don't just delay.
Skills we've honed, minds set free,
Choose companions carefully.

Everyday wisdom whispers clearly,
The journey's end is always near.
Close this book with heart and mind,
Embrace the world, be gentle, be kind.

For in each line, and every page,
Lies a story, a truth, a sage.
Feel the warmth, the hope, the light,
You've conquered much, now take flight!